Theory and Practical
Instruction
in the
Book of Thoth

Etteilla
(Jean-Baptiste Alliette)

Theory and Practical
Instruction
on the
Book of Thoth

or about the higher power, of nature and man,
to dependably reveal the mysteries of life
and to give oracles according to the
wondrous art of the Egyptians

Etteilla
(Jean-Baptiste Alliette)

translated by Kerry A Nitz
from the unattributed
German translation

K A Nitz
AUCKLAND, NEW ZEALAND

ISBN: 978-0-473-62400-2

Theoretischer und praktischer
Unterricht über das Buch Thot — neue Auflage
published in German 1857 (first edition 1793)
in an unattributed translation with additions
(possibly by Etteilla's student Hisler)
of the original French of 1790:
Cours théorique et pratique du livre de Thot:
pour entendre avec justesse l'art, la science
et la sagesse de rendre les oracles

ISBN: 978-0-473-62400-2

Translator's Foreword

Etteilla, the pseudonym of Jean-Baptiste Alliette (1738–1791), was a French occultist who first widely popularised the use of the tarot for divination and who coined the term cartomancy. The tarot deck he used, known as Etteilla's Book of Thoth or the Grand Etteilla, was specifically designed for use in divination. It differs in key respects to more recent tarot decks (such as the Rider-Waite deck which was influenced by it), particularly in the major arcana, and the following text relies on possession of such a deck.

Preface

I offer my fellow living men samples of a science which was worshipped so sacredly by the first wise men of humanity within the walls of their temples, but was ignored and neglected by their later offspring, a science which is deeply interwoven with the borders of philosophy, and which is deeply related to the area of knowledge of the entire universe.

It was in the early years of my life that I was once stumbling around in the gray treasures of antiquity — and finding the sacred remains of this science, inquired into it, discovered in it the source of virtue and the knowledge of God — and that I now, after many years of experience, after worried lonely nights, am also sharing with my fellow men and women the light that appeared for me. My effort will be misjudged, my wish, good people, to lead you to the true source of virtue will be rewarded with ingratitude, or it won't! I have nothing to fear — only a few steps yet and I am in the place of rest and in the sleep where ingratitude does not disturb me nor worry me. But I wish and hope that a few might like to follow me and take this science into their heart, adopt it as a late offspring and also fill themselves with joy by it. Indeed honour it, this science, step with blessed brow into its temple — listen though to the call whereby I would like to assure you and lead you on this path as a fortunate traveller! —

Do not be shocked when you stumble here and there on thorny bushes, impassable ways, steep rocks and cliffs — above them you will come upon glorious views, delightful scenes and landscapes. Do not be shocked, I say, when you find in specific parts of the teaching which I present to you at first appearance incomprehensible parts, incredible words — only a short time will pass, and it will become easy for you —

just for a short time spare no effort to study them, and it will all be cleared up so that you find the deep treasure of wisdom and taste it.

Secondly take the guide which I give you as company on your travels by the hand intimately and in a friendly way! It will strengthen you with its stimulating balm, clamber with you over the thorny path, climb with you the steep rocks. — The 78 cards or the Book of Thoth is this guide — just do not forsake it, and you will never go astray — take it always by the hand and you will never stumble upon paths which cannot be climbed over.

Thirdly I will also myself support you from time to time with my advice, with my help, hover about you like a good friend if you appreciate my effort to always be around you and lead you. I mean I will seek, if you are satisfied with these samples which I deliver from this science, to give you still more light into these mysteries, let you even deeper into these mysteries, through new samples, through new writings, and lead you to higher knowledge.

Examine *everything* and seek! — The path on which you travel is not blissful, but glorious is the outlook which you will obtain on it.

The author.

First Lesson in the Egyptian Art of Oracle Giving

First Drawing

The Book of Thoth, or what that namely is, the book which concerns God, mankind, and nature, is gathered together in 78 drawn hieroglyphic figures.

Have you, oh human, fathomed these depths, have you arrived in the innermost part of the sanctuary to place in order these many figures that speak importantly, to place them as the old wise men understood to order them according to their sacred mystical language[1]: then you have, fortunate one!, climbed to the highest degree of the wisdom on which once Tris Merkurius Athotis stood, thus you can proclaim with the pious virtuous Moor, as he said to King Khalid, "Whoever has everything, needs nothing more."

Oh! Your only truly consecrated ones of the natural philosophy who by rights do not allow that God becomes reconciled through faith without works, or through prayer without work; they stir themselves for pity, which you cannot rightly believe, that through a foolish invocation, which mocks both human as well as divine reason, demons must be forced to expose the secrets of nature to man, to unveil them to him —

---

1   The old wise men, especially of the Orient and in Egypt, had a doubled speech and a doubled way of writing — one which served them in everyday life, and another for the recording of their philosophy and nature wisdom, which existed in hieroglyphic signs and figures.

you, I say, come here, open this Book of Thoth, and look! — It supports your faith, it confirms your principles.

Here you will find how the fanatical, so-called Illuminati hope in vain for the revelation of the mysteries from the lips of the highest, how this science is strewn around only in the individual works of the universe whose obtaining they always expect in vain by direct divine inspiration.

Yes, we must seek in the individual parts of creation, search for it; we must not, as those careless spontaneous men did, flatter ourselves that by sudden miracle the Godhead will put in our hands the key to the door to nature, as those unfortunates think who are still happy enough in themselves that they do not dare to clamber themselves after God's wisdom.

Here you will at the same time learn from this sublime Book how far human understanding goes astray, how much others, in contrast to those idiots who possess enough baseness of the soul, are struck again by hellish spirits, enemies of the Godhead, enemies of mankind and all nature, the reward of their effort being to hope for a happiness which is only offered to them in the way all crimes believing in good luck, all crimes carelessly committed are.

Oh! Friends, seek that sacred hidden wisdom according to the will of God, according to the ever lively urge in your breast for the traces of nature, that wisdom which was planted by the creator in the first germs of all beings, do you distrust my gesture when I call to you, *"Come, open the Book of Thoth, you will find!"* — No, do not distrust me — my age, my experience, the untiring search, my office itself, to peer into the corners of the human heart, has allowed me to find your true education to get to know God, nature, itself, allowed me to find the education which you have never yet found and acquired with all your efforts.

Yes! Study in the divine Book of Thoth, in the book of God, of mankind and of nature what true wise men among the first Egyptians recorded. — Wise men who, not corrupted by the taste for trivial arts, for restive stormy passions, turned all their time to perceiving this great trinity — God, mankind and nature. This trinity is still unfamiliar to us, without knowledge of which though, mingling truth with error, error with truth is unavoidable.

But I hear already how you, ever accustomed to being deceived by con men, ask me distrustfully whom I place as guarantor for my honesty, as guarantor for this well-intentioned advice? — then listen! — it is *Trismegistus* himself who gives you this teaching, this advice — Trismegistus whom you could not possibly reject, since he places himself as guarantor for you. —

Open the Book of Thoth — and among the thousand divine beauties his prayer will shine towards you straightaway at the first glimpse on the first card — his prayer —

God, I desire to be acquainted with the things which are around me — — desire to understand what they are — and to understand what you yourself are.

The science of numbers is the principal cause of all higher knowledge. It is very easy and simple to understand and see them before all others. You need do nothing but steer your mind to ethics, to become acquainted with them, and to comprehend them; for ethics and the science of numbers are one and the same. Take, for example, the sentence: *the highest or the uppermost is like the lowest*; with the physical knowledge the physical truths are proven $2 + 2 = 4$.

God is 1.

From this truth which the unjust or mad denier of God makes into a nothing, into a nullity, the idol worshipper in contrast though wants to make into a greater number — from this unity, I say, flows, in reference to our Book of Thoth, the first trinity. —

1 namely; the wise person who sees into the future and in prophesying unveils its mysteries; 2, the one thirsting for knowledge who strives to learn the destiny of his life from the former; and 3, all humanity, all living and lifeless beings which link to the chain of destinies in the life of that person who is thirsting for knowledge and asking after the mysteries of the future.

Oh! You questioning, noble, thirster after knowledge who hopes rightly to learn the destiny of your life — but even you, unknowing, careless, you who have not armed yourself against the blows of the future with care and foresight — do you not see that I must call out here all the infinite causes which, to your fortune or misfortune, lie in ambush? — Yes —

hear it! — it is only foresight, the foresight which can avert the fall of a tile from your head, protect your foot from the blow of a stone.

Certainly there is a science of foreseeing. But it is also only a fruit of long years, of long experience and of deep and sharp understanding. There is a science of forecasting! — A science, however, which is only acquired when you have fathomed all other human knowledge — for on this it supports itself, if I at most exclude the science which a single true God teaches us to know. — But now back again to the thread of the lesson! —

1. Imagine here the strong sublime human, 2. the weak impotent person and 3. can you imagine and picture the *strong* and *weak* person — when he is strong then the questioning thirster of knowledge can promise themselves fortunate events; but when he is weak, the querent[1] has nothing but misfortune to fear. —

As in the first outline of creation and the elements of the entire number system, we now also seek here for a fourth — and it is the *Book of Thoth* which immediately reveals itself as the sought-for fourth, and which at the same time, seen as a whole, as one book, brings to mind the unity 1.

From this whole, from this unity of the Book of Thoth, however, now flows a new trinity which, however, is surely subordinate to the above (namely to the strong person, to the weak person, and to the sometimes strong, sometimes weak). Since namely the unity 1 of the Book of Thoth from which we want to derive that trinity is only the type and the idea of divine unity, then now too this unity 1 is — in that the Book of Thoth contains the science of the entire universe in itself — compiled from 78 cards. This compilation, however, now gives us that trinity in that it gives opportunity to the wise unveiler of the future and to he who inquires and asks of it accordingly.

1. To shuffle the cards, 2. to then cut them, and 3. to again place alongside each other and combine the two parties or parts which arise from the opening, from the cutting of the Book of Thoth. Note here at the same time how the strong

---

1   [Tr.: the term of querent has been used for the one consulting the oracle throughout this translation.]

person[1], in that he always brings the Book again to the unity 1, must oppose the will of the weak person[2], in that the latter always endeavours to place the Book in the number 2, in two parts, but I will talk further of that below.

You will ask, who, however, will now bring out the number four from which this arises? From the division of the Book in three rows, if you lay the entire Book in three rows, I answer you, and if you namely then, as you must do, direct your attention always to the middle row and use it.

The unveiler of the future namely, if he now wants to penetrate into its mysteries and decipher them for the other person, first shuffles the 78 cards so that he, so long as he shuffles them, does not look at them; then puts down the Book or the cards in order to have them cut by the querent, and finally allocates the 78 cards, or the entire Book in three rows so that in each row 26, the first trinity 26, 26, 26. 0, when the picture of the circle lies there before him.

Whereupon he takes the 26 cards which lie in the middle row, and puts them to the side to his right. Then takes up again the two remaining rows lying there 26, 0, 26, which make 52 cards all up, and follows the same rules with them which we have given, so that he namely shuffles, has cut, and then places in three rows. In this way the third trinity, 17, 17, 17, + 1 then arises by this second procedure as the image of unity.

For the third time finally, after he has previously withdrawn the middle row of 17, and has placed them to the side next to the 26, he again takes up the remaining rows 17, 0, 17, 1, which makes 35, and follows with them the same procedure. Thus the third trinity of the Book of Thoth appears, 11, 11, 11, +2, as next to the represented image of the human.

After this third and last division of the Book of Thoth, his reckoning table or the Book of Thoth lies before him there in the following order:

11, 0, 11, 2, ... 11, 17, 26.

---

1   The strong person is namely, as was explained already above, he who reveals the future from the cards, from the Book of Thoth.

2   The weak person is he who asks about the future, and begs those (the strong) for the unveiling.

How much now urges me not to tell! — The language to suppress that urge and to describe everything must be subject to the swift ability to think. But we will try.

26 has reference and connection with the first procedure of laying the Book of Thoth and telling the future from the same. 17 relates to the second procedure, and 11 to the third time of the procedure of the art of division.

When we want to know what numbers appear at the fourth and fifth time of laying the cards and stand in relation to these, then we may only look back at the remaining cards from the third division of the Book of Thoth. The number of them next to the number two, which did not come into the row on the third and last division, can easily find us the fourth number after the proper procedure. And so we can also easily arrive at the fifth and last number if we proceed here, as for the fourth time, with the division of the cards.

But before we now continue, we must for a few moment direct our minds at the union of souls and spirits — so that the correspondence of them, which is necessary if thorough, sacred oracle shall flow from the mouth of the unveiler, may be established and joined up the more easily and intimately.

From where, however, you ask, shall we recognise this correspondence of spirits, whether it is established or not? — How can and should we believe in the union of them? —

I come to the most important thing. The blazing flames of the fire seek themselves, cling to each other in order to mutually enliven each other — the youthful bodies of humans urge for the deepest union of sensation; and you shall not allow that the ever active, never shackled, strongest, most soulful spirit seeks its like, fuses mutually with it into one, and feels mutual delight and pleasure in the stream of emanating being? What would be external to nature! What would be the hope which wings its way from me to God, to the second image of my soul, to the wife of creation, if my soul lay shackled in the prison of the body!

No, it must be easy for you to believe in union of the spirits, and correspondence of the same! Only it depends on you recognising whether it is established or not — only it depends at the same time, however, on your will and on the arts of skill and purity of the unveiler of the future to cause this union.

If the unveiler of the future, for example, does not have the virtues which are given below, then it is impossible that the union of souls should happens of itself. He is then like a wolf who roams about in sheep's clothing in order to tear apart the flock. The questioning thirster for knowledge then recognises immediately that the correspondence is not established when the unveiler says something which does not enter into the past, present, or future.

But in order to pull off the union of spirits and the correspondence between the unveiler of the future and the querent, it is thus necessary that the former really has the intention, the will to heal, and that in the former the belief in being healed really is dominant. For the gods and nature are never deaf towards righteous voices which call them. You must, however, also, so that everything is observed, turn in your thoughts both to God and also to mankind and nature, and to always have the lively faith in your disposition that God can in fact do everything He wants.

The questioning thirster for knowledge of the mysteries of the future can rightly call to account the false unveiler of the same over the mangling of the mutual union of spirit, and complain to him when the chain of his life's destiny is not revealed. With full right though, however, the true unveiler of the future can damn the false hypocritical querent because he can moreover see from the Book of Thoth what the cause is, what has hindered the correspondence. But now it remains to us to cite the moments when the correspondence first begins, when it fuses together perfectly into one, and when it is finally animated and received, and by what.

With the first cutting or the opening of the Book of Thoth, which happens by the querent, the correspondence begins by itself to gradually be established. With the second opening or cutting of the same the spirits seek to unite with one another and to merge. With the third cutting finally this transition is complete, and the spirits really are fused with one another. The remaining times that the querent cuts and opens the Book of Thoth (which is only possible four times), serves merely for maintaining this fusing of spirit, and always to enliven and renew the action and reaction of the spirits. Here, audience! Pay close attention to what happens in the faces of the magical person and the true querent and what picture is painted there ... !! — But we will return again to our sublime magical table.

11, 0, 11, 2, ... 11, 17, 26.

It is impossible for the unveiler of the future with all his skill, all his wisdom and purity of heart, to give from the unity of the Book of Thoth all the wise information and oracle to the querent. He follows hence the great example of the divine author of all things who drew forth from his unity the first three elements[1] for the creation of all beings, and according to the pattern of this great master makes in a quite sublime way a similar trinity from the Book of Thoth[2]. If though he now already dissects this first trinity of the Book and places it in rows, he thus receives finally from this *triple* trinity[3] a trinity, namely 11, 17, 26. As discharge from the whole, 11, 0, 11, 2 remains to him, as in the chaos of creation the earth was also the discharge from fire, air and water.

If you direct your thoughts attentively to the sublime division of the cards of the Book of Thoth, as it has namely proceeded, you will surely notice that the Book, which consists of 78 cards, has given 54 ternaries[4], so that also according to the same the ternarium, the trinity 11, 17, 26 appears now finally in newly visible rows, and the victory is retained!

Do not finally let anything at all of the sublime beauties of these secret numbers be lost, you will be still more astounded when you see that through the placement and ordering of the six times nine trinities and by the + 1 + 2 the seven trinities are created[5].

As the giver of the oracle cannot unveil the future from the direct unity 1 of the Book of Thoth, he is just as incapable of this from the number of persons 2, which the querent always

---

1 The first elements and original matter of creation were namely fire, air and water.

2 In that namely the inquiring unveiler of the future places the Book of Thoth in three rows of 26, 26, 26.

3 The prophesying human places the Book three times in three rows, namely firstly the 78 cards, for the second time the 52, for the third time the 35, and each time in three rows. This is called the triple trinity.

4 The trinity 11, 17, 26 namely added up gives 54.

5 The seven trinities are namely 11, 0, 11, 2, ... 11, 17, 26.

holds up and offers to the magical person through the opening of the unity of the Book into two parts.

The book must thus be divided into three parts. And this repeated three times is the true mysterious sublime work, in view of how the entire creation happened, and in view of the number 26 over which we must be astonished. Everything in the Book of Thoth has its intention and its significance.

The entire Book 1 is the single number of the Godhead — 78 the number of melac or salt, the indestructible spirit; 26 the number of the greatest most sublime name of the Godhead, *Jeova.*

With the first laying of the 78 cards none remain; that means that nothing remains. This nothing is denoted by a null, and the 0 is the figure of the circle 0.

With the second laying of the 54 cards, 17 came into each row, but 1 was left over. This 1 is the point for the centre of the circle, and represents the Godhead in the middle of the extent of the circumference.

With the third laying, 11 came into each row, and 2 remained, that is the person who is denoted by this number. The former thus and the latter represents for us the Godhead in the centres of the person, the man and the woman; or the fire, the spirit, the soul of the universe in the middle of the white woman and the black man — as you could see on the 14th card of the Book of Thoth which you must have before your eye.

The magical giver of the oracle is not capable of splitting the number of the unity 1, nor also of the number of the name 26 which signifies Jeova. But he must analyse the number 17 in its parts in order to find 10 as the circle of Godhead, secondly the 4 as the idea of knowledge of nature, and thirdly the 3 as the idea of human wisdom.

The number 11 also cannot be further split and analysed. It indicates only that before 11 is the number 10, and that after 11 comes the number 12. That is the actual relationship as if in smaller numbers the 1 multiplied gives 2, and this divided again the halves of the same; the halves, however, and the 2 do not signify the Godhead; 10 thus and 17 are more sublime and stronger than 11.

11 is the sign of the weakness of the person, and at the same time, if you take the opposite of human weakness, the sign of divine power and strength.

It is thus above all necessary that the student of the wisdom of the Book of Thoth understand and know this — 1 as the point in the centre; 2 as the woman and the man, etc. Now again to our magical table of numbers!

11, 0, 11, 2, ... 11, 17, 26.

26 is the image of the soul; 17 the image of the intellect, and 11 the image of the body; for, as the majority of those initiates of the art say, thus our philosopher's stone also has, just as the human, soul, intellect and body.[1]

From the union of these three substances arises now the life which is represented by the number 24, the number left remaining in this form 11, 11, 2.

These remarks and these numbers 26, 17, 11 and 24 are now for the magical giver of the oracle the most precious discoveries next to all those which he has already made, and which are unfamiliar to you. In that he now namely represents the entire Book of Thoth in four parts 26, 17, 11, 11 + 11, he finds that the fourth part of the Book, 11 + 11, according to the hieroglyphs, is greater than all the remaining three parts of the Book — for 26, 17, 11, 2 = 56 is just the number which the fourth part of the Book of Thoth, considered hieroglyphically, comes to.

Furthermore he also finds in the number 17 something strange — for according to the hieroglyphs the first and second part of the Book of Thoth makes exactly 17 cards, and the third part of the same makes 5 cards.

Now lay down the Book of Thoth separately before you — you will find that the Book is a whole which, continuing from 1 to 77 cards, finally with the card that is marked with a null, consists of 78 cards.

This number 78, which is pyramidal and similar to a triangle, proves to me now that the 3 represents the spirit of the Book of Thoth. I say thus that 3 is the spirit, 1 the soul and 78 the body of the Book of Thoth.

---

1   [Tr.: this paragraph is potentially significant for interpreting the cards in each row.]

The four divisions which make up all sciences, e.g. philosophy, theology, medicine, jurisprudence, and takes place in them, gives me now also a 4.

Likewise the Book of Thoth also becomes strange in view of its number 7, over which I am now yet more astonished; 7 times 11 cards namely, the card with the null also taken into account, makes the entirety of the Book.

Indeed from all sides this 7 which we find in the Book of Thoth must amaze us, for even itself in the 78 from which it is composed, the 7 imposes itself on our eyes. —

Because thus in all figures, the 7 itself always lies hidden and contained in the whole; thus I establish the following table, 1, 2, 3, 4, 5, 6, 7.

From the Book of Thoth, in so far as it is a unity in its entirety, I derive the number 1.

From the four divisions of the Book in 26, 17, 11, ... 11 + 11 + 2 the number 4.

From the strange seven finally, which contains perhaps still more wonder and greatness within itself than the entirety of the Book, and the 4 divisions, I derive the number 7.

This gives me thus cause for these two tables; 1, 4, 7, ... 2, 3, 5, 6. Here I must, however, now surely ask, when I take consideration of the spirit of the Book, what 3 is; why there aren't three tables, or why the table does not consist of three parts? — And here I see myself forced now thus to an entirely natural operation which agrees entirely with the constant cutting of the Book of Thoth in two parts. Set down namely the table 1, 4, 7. Here you find that 1 + 7 = 8, and the half of that is 4. Set thus, since also 2 + 6 = 8, and the half is 4, this 4 under that 4; furthermore since also 3 + 5 = 8, and the half is 4, this 4 again under that 4; and thus you receive a single table whose spirit is the 3.

1, 4, 7 = 12 as the cards of the first part of the Book.

$$\begin{array}{r} 4 \\ \underline{4} \\ 12 \end{array}$$

If you now make an expanded table of the 1, 4, 7 = 12; in that you add together the first twelve numbers, 1, 2, 3, 4, 5, 6, 7, 8, 9, 10, 11, 12 = 78; then you receive to your astonishment the full number of cards of which the Book of Thoth consists.

Oh! You reverer of all higher knowledge and especially of hermetic philosophy, which is the only true science of nature; for which you acquire at great cost other useless profane volumes and writings! — Come here, and draw here for some time from the true wells of wisdom!

Second Lesson

Second Drawing

In my first lesson I have, according to the example of the Egyptian wise men and one of their students, the great lawgiver of the Hebrews, sought to make clear and prove that you do not have to have the faith and the pride, as if you could directly obtain from God the key to the mysteries of nature, that you also, however, do not have to lower yourself so much as to call up hellish spirits and conjure them to the discovery of the future.

The Godhead has indeed put the key in our hands which unlocks the garden of all nature for us; but this key is not a direct gift, rather the means with which God has outfitted us to recognise and distinguish evil from good.

Revelation is a direct gift. Not everyone can boast of them; but rather they are preserved only for those who can penetrate into the divine disclosures and who know how to unveil them. It would be foolishness of humans, and vain arrogance, to request the honour, the gift of being unveiler of the divine oracle and mysteries!

Indeed in the centre of the immeasurable garden in which God has placed us — but not in the heaven or in the hell from which the Godhead has kept us distant — is where we must seek after and inquire into this science. Senses and reason are our guides to lead and steer us on this path of nature.

Likewise it is also a proof of the greatest ignorance when you want to attribute to God the control of the smallest human act as it were. Otherwise would not also the tone which the hammer brings forth on the bell have to be a work of control by the divine hand?

No! Only God has created the entire universe, and the law written down in it — *that we shall find everything when we react to it and strive after it.*

With the first steps of my thirst for knowledge, it is now almost forty years, I had also fallen into those stupidities — with increasing years, however, I have learnt not to resist the reason and the natural knowledge which stirred in me, and which called me to my present mysteries.

Yet other people, outside those Illuminati and those conjurors of spirits — people who were usually skilful, but not initiated into the higher knowledge — held it to be a duty to convince me that the giving of oracles and the foreseeing of the future were nothing but chimera and fantasy. Their sophisms and conclusions did not deceive me though; *here,* I said to them, *know what has met you, and what now stands before you and will meet you tomorrow.* And thus I refuted them by the inspection.

Astonished over the truth and certainty of the art of telling the future in advance, they now wanted to take their refuge in empty excursions — an accident, they said, the chance it is certain characters which make it come true. But I have revealed and stated previously to you about certain events which do not depend on accident, I answered. — Yes, that is true! — No scholar, there is no danger in the world, everything is linked, everything is chained together in order! But you must study this linkage, this ordering of the chain, and you will be unveiler of the future, unveiler of the past and of the present! —

But, without extending myself further over it, I just say, human, you are here below in this world to observe the work of the creator and to imitate his divine wisdom — it is your will constantly, constantly your work to make miracles as it was the work of the Godhead always to bring forth and give existence to miracles.

But in order to possess the knowledge of nature which is the mental capacity of every human, you must have studied nature. Then you need neither a divine inspiration, nor a hellish conjuring of spirits; you need only be a friend of man-kind, a connoisseur of nature.[1]

You have learnt in my first lesson now that the science of numbers is the principal knowledge of numbers, like arith-metic as well, without contradiction certainly the principle one of all the sciences which we possess.

Secondly you have learnt that the knowledge of numbers is at the same time the easiest and simplest of all knowledge — that the science of numbers is one and the same with ethics. Over this I have told you, in order to vanquish your disbelief if you were dominated by it, that all ethics with the entire sci-ence of numbers consists in the unity 1; but that you, because you can extract no knowledge from the straight unity, must take your refuge in the great trinity — in the trinity namely — *God — humanity — and nature.*

Let us now open the book of nature, at the same time though also think of the book of the philosophers', of the Book of Thoth; for in this the great work of the creation of nature, the great masterpiece — the human, and finally in hu-manity the great work of the Godhead is written and drawn.

If you now think of a sphere as the idea of the entire uni-verse, then this sphere will also, if you raise your mind still further and push forward with it, be the idea, the image of di-vine unity itself. When we climb down from the cause to its effects, the sphere will finally also become the idea of human-ity, of nature, and even the image of the entire Book of Thoth.

We may now think of and look on this sphere as a figure in a particular way — thus will the centre of it represent the mid-point of nature. In the centre of this midpoint will be the hu-man, and in the midpoint of humanity the Godhead.

When we thus consider according to this established basis the human as placed in the centre of the sphere, then his head will show and reveal the zenith, and his feet the nadir.

When his eyes radiate from these two points, he can de-scribe a semicircle. To complete this semicircle, however, he must take refuge in his mind, that is, in the higher knowledge.

---

1   [Tr.: the German translation omits a large section of the French edition here.]

This first circle shall be called the equator; the second, which he can describe with the tips of his fingers, the meridian; and finally the third, of which he has drawn one part with the senses, the other part in thought, the horizon.

These three circles are now completely sufficient to prove and make clear everything in the higher sciences and human knowledge — it must not be less, however, for the trinity is entirely necessary for the discovery and for the finding of truth. Now we want to go on to talk comprehensibly for everybody, and put off expressing it geometrically for another time.

If you now describe these three greater circles, which are themselves in view of the form of the earth correct and true, on the sphere, what important things are to be found there! —

God as the unity which gives a trinity; man as a compilation of soul, spirit and body; nature as an existence of salt, sulphur, mercury; the Book of Thoth in its various parts as 22, the greatest, 16, the smallest number of all, and 40 more insignificant cards. Thus also in the arithmetic the number 3 as made from the even and odd; in geometry the three measures, height, length, breadth.

These three parts, 22, 16, 40, could they not be that which you call the physical spirit of the Book of Thoth? Indeed it is.

The sphere, or the world 1 gave opportunity for the origin of the Book of Thoth — 3 constituted the spirit of the latter and former; and 7, as Cicero said, is the key and the explanation for everything.

But before we continue, it is now necessary that we above all find the number which signifies nature. Can you though surely fail to recognise it in the number of four divisions which we find in every science and which we have mentioned above?[1] — Now, however, we want to take the sphere in hand again in that we do not ever refrain from applying it to the Book of Thoth. For the sphere is the image of nature, and the Book of Thoth is also nature because it was described and written down by the first wise men according to nature.

How though shall the great number 5, or the Godhead in the centre of the four main points, and the four main ele-

---

1   You will recall of what was said about it above — that e.g. philosophy, theology, medicine, jurisprudence — are all in fours.

ments from which the universe took its existence, be comprehended in the sphere? — Like the 22, among all numbers the greatest — like the 4 divisions of each thing? — In the point of the centre of the sphere, I answer, in the midpoint of the four points of the horizontal circle. Indeed you must, I answer, confirm and establish for yourself this centre in the middle of a perfect number 6.

The sections of this circle form 7 points:

1) the zenith where the Godhead is.

1) the centre of the universe where the human is placed.

1) the nadir where nature is.

4) the four cardinal points $1 + 1 + 1 + 4 = 7$.

When you give a human, in view of the 7 points of the sphere, seven higher sciences, then he is thus the greatest cabalist. When you show a geometer seven points in the circle, then he will have arrived on the trail of discovery of all mathematical truths; and finally when you give one of the representatives of the French nation in their National Assembly[1] seven virtues, then in seven days France will blossom into the garden of Eden which was on earth before Adam's fall and the lasciviousness of Eve. And why? Because the number seven 7 is the key to all things, and because, as a hermetical philosopher rightly said, you need the key to both unlock and lock.

You thus always have the Book of Thoth in your thoughts, and you find that 1 is God; 2 humanity — man and woman (none, however, may have a hidden ambiguity of hermaphroditic form in themselves); 3 the basic elements of nature; 4 the elements of all things and sciences; and finally 7 the key to all knowledge which is preserved for the wise in nature.

God is surrounded in the middle of the sphere by 6 radii or rays. 6 is the first perfect number for the geometers, as 28 is the second perfect number. The wise Egyptians thought thus in that manner already four thousand years ago as the Book of Thoth shows.

The highest number of points which 3 circles described on a sphere brings forth is, including the point of the centre, 7. If

---

1   Fortune of misfortune! The current representatives in the convention seem to have found or lost the seven virtues.

you in fact cut the sphere or a lemon in three circles, then you would have the seven points and at the same time the number 8, for 7 and 8 make, as you surely know, 78, the number of cards of the Book of Thoth. This is again a proof for you of how this sublime book in every consideration was drawn up with the deepest knowledge of God, of nature, of humanity and numbers.

But what will all this just amount to when you find the subtle working out of the number 78 which according to the hieroglyphs rises up to 360, and which will again be divided without remainder!

With that we now arrive though all the more easily at the simple instructions of our second lesson; thus we want to set down now the three parts with the remainders 24, ... 11, 17, 16, which came out of our procedure.

26...1
17...1
11..1
24

Read here from the right hand to the left, as you also had to place the cards of the Book thus in rows, from 1 to 26, from 1 to 17, and thirdly from 1 to 11.

Since now 26 is the soul, 17 the intellect and 11 the body of the Book, thus 24 is also understood to be life, which is indicated by the remainder, so that you should not consider the explanations and oracle which you find in the three rows alone to be entirely certain and unmistakeable. But you must recite and proclaim everything out loud as you see it before you.

If the cards marked 1 and 8 are found in the same row, then it is a sign that the one who asks you is married.

If the card 1 appears right-away in the first placement, at position I of the first line or row, then it is certain that virtue has won the war over sensuality with regards namely to the one who is asking you.

When by contrast the card 1 appears elsewhere in position 26 of the first row, then the passions are wielding the sceptre over virtue.

If the number 1 does not appear for a male querent (for a female querent it must be the 8) in the placement of the 26, then you have to foretell that the querent is not on the right path of fortune and virtue. And you must report to him, since you should be his spiritual doctor, his illness and the remedy here at the same time.

You can almost always see the type of illness from the first of the 26 cards. The remedy is, however, more or less distantly indicated in the fifth time of placing the cards of the Book of Thoth — in general it must, however, reveal itself at best in the fourth time of placing them.

When the 8 falls alone (with a male querent namely) in the row of 26 cards, then tell him that the woman who interests the querent most of all sees more correctly than him, or that she is at least more attentive to the fortune, the house and the good behaviour of the querent.

Card 1, the inquirer, may now appear amidst the cards in the rows, or not; thus you must think of it at the start of each row, and at the start of each unveiling of the future. But if it falls in the first place, position I of the 26, then tell the querent that he has the ability and mind to direct the same in himself and to think about what interests him and is close to his heart.

The oracle giver must say with a loud, certain, articulate and slow voice everything he is capable of finding shown in the artwork in the mysteriously significant cards. But when he does not have enough comprehensive knowledge to precisely and certainly note and keep present the signs, the characteristics and meanings from the first time of placing the cards up to the last time, then he must write them down. For only from the whole of the five times of placing the cards and by proper and orderly notice of the sequence, of the positional circumstances, can and must the entire fabric of explanations and signs be formed and determined.

The one who possess up to the fourth[1] degree in this art of giving oracle from the cards grasps, in the midst of the multitude of objects which force themselves before him, correctly and precisely every reference, every relationship, in order to form from them a binding chain of life coincidences and to hold them before the querent in binding order.

---

1   [Tr.: the original French refers to the third degree, as the German translation also does two paragraphs below.]

But anyone who loses the thread of his observations, he is like that one who has forgotten the consequence of cause and effect. In this case a correct sequence of life events is impossible.

Art, science and human wisdom unite together in the hieroglyphic signs of the Book of Thoth. The true unveiler of the future who has penetrated as far as the third degree of his art always follows the tracks of nature, and finds them thus lying naked as it were unveiled before himself. To skilfully comprehend everything which he finds on its path, he does not mutilate it like the false giver of oracles who cunningly entices from the querent his life circumstances and secrets.

Certainly no human can deserve the name of a great man who knows nothing of the delights of the soul which the philosopher enjoys in his cabinet when, surrounded by his mute, motionless, deaf friends, the hieroglyphs, he understands the voices which give him the Godhead, nature and humanity in them.

Since I have now given you instruction over the explanation of the first placing of cards, as I will also do so in even more detail further below, you must now, in that you always keep the meanings of the first placing of cards precisely in your memory, gather up the 78 cards or the entire Book again in order to place the cards for the second time.

So shuffle the cards again with averted face; have them cut — and then place a row of 17 cards in that you always take away one card after the other from the entire book:

17...1

But now look at the 18th card which lies on the Book, as well as the 78th, as the last of the Book.

The viewing of these two cards, which alone the first wise men allowed us, lets us now find out two things:

1. how the querent is disposed towards the wise unveiler of the future, what he has in his heart for him;
2. what the cause is when the correspondence was not established at the first cutting.

If I thus discover that the one who is asking me is not entirely in correspondence with me, then the 18th and the 78th card give me the cause for it. At the same time, however, the same cards – the correspondence between me and the querent may also be yet be so little and tiny — also uncover for me what the querent thinks of me. Thus you can see two things from one thing at the same time.

The unveiler of the future thinks precisely about these two cards, the 18th and 78th, for they are the only means of preservation which the wise men have lent him for watching out for the snares which can be placed both undeservedly and maliciously for him.

These 17 cards which comprise the entire second procedure of placing the cards must be taken one after the other from the Book of Thoth so that the first card of the book also appears at position I, in that you begin to place the cards from right to left, 17 ... 1.

When the row is now placed, then the oracle giver (which he must always observe with each row) must place the 17th card in the place of the 1st card to his right, and the 1st card in the place of the 17th to his left. This is called *drawing again* 1, 17; 2, 16; 3, 15; etc., for the cards to the right hand of the oracle giver must always be placed to his left, and thus be read from the right to the left.

Any time when the number of cards in a row is odd, the middle card — after the *redrawing* has happened — is thrown to the side as remainder, because it has no card which is parallel to it.

But before we now continue further in our second lesson, we want to consider beforehand an important circumstance.

It is namely with the correspondence of the spirits the question whether it really, since it cannot be comprehended by our minds, although already hundreds of examples from experience prove it, whether it really, I say, sets beyond all doubt that the Book of Thoth can give oracle and explanation.

When namely the oracle giver wants to claim that he knows how to read in the Book of Thoth all events of life in their order, and if and where they happened or will happen, then he must not only prove that a correspondence between him and the querent has taken place, a correspondence between the Book of Thoth, the querent and him as the oracle giver at the same time, rather he must also demonstrate that a correspondence, a far-reaching connection between all animate and inanimate beings has taken place, which during the

life of the querent determines all those fortunate or unfortunate events whose unfortunate victim he becomes, or whose
object he is to his fortune.

The correspondence in general of those individual parts
and individual connections in at times ethical or intellectual,
or at times physical consideration are, however, not only as
numerous, but rather a hundred thousand times more difficult to determine and to set apart than the countless changes
which the 78 cards of the Book of Thoth suffer in their situ-
ation. What secrets do not prevail here! Take your refuge in
the book of wisdom, in the Book of Thoth.

Indeed in this book you will find described not only the
science, the art, the deep wisdom of the unveiler of the future,
not only the various situations which are possible between the
78 cards of the Book of Thoth, not only the various phenom-
ena, causes, and effects of correspondence, but rather also
everything that a faithful description, a faithful true picture of
the whole interconnectedness of our universe can deliver to
you.

But in order to not believe that you are in the universe like
a ship as it were which is tossed about by the waves sometimes hither, sometimes thither, I must say to all those who
understand me and the Book that the basis for everything
which you find in the book rests in its connection to the 26
letters of the alphabet.

But in order to finally also convince the scholars themselves that it is worth dedicating yourself with every effort to
the science of the Book of Thoth, I say the following.

Our 26 letters have no other property in themselves than
that of forming words, those words becoming small hieroglyphs from which and by which you can put together entire
speeches. These hieroglyphs constitute the entire science of
our Book of Thoth.

It follows from that that our present letters are no longer
those of the old peoples.

The hieroglyphs of the Book of Thoth are already in themselves hieroglyphic. Equipped with the proper knowledge,
you can just as little fail to recognise their synonyms and
homonyms as you can with knowledge of grammar find the
synonyms of our language incomprehensible.

Third Lesson

Third Drawing

By what misfortune do all knowledge, arts, sciences, all the parts of nature itself which have the intention of advancing the highest fortune of humanity contain the cause of that misery, the basis of its misfortune?

From the unity of one God, from the pure simple ethics which the Godhead itself planted in the souls of the first humans, as it is now still there and found in the true adepts of the hermetic philosophy, arose the majority of the gods, the idolatry and the fanaticism which plagues our time.

From the natural knowledge which is also the most important to humanity there arose through ignorant people every possible error and fallacy which in the end led even learned men to doubt the necessity and usefulness of the sciences and the arts.

In that these remarks force themselves on me, and they moreover convince me that the false and incorrect *art of placing the cards* only arose out of the true way which the chain of human fates teaches us to find, what fear must I now not be scared of, since I am writing down a science and giving to the present day what the first Egyptian wise men had invented in order to bring all sciences to the stage of completion which is extremely necessary for the fortunes of humanity? —

But what! — Because trust opens the doors to the thief, I should as a fearful man conceal the science — not reveal the art to my fellow men, to posterity — the art without which, I confess and maintain, nobody can be completely happy? —

Yes, in order to put aside all dispute that anyone who does not understand the sublime Egyptian art of oracle giving is extremely unfortunate, I need only prove that it is that which orders and forms the human mind, that it is that which deserves to be called *the art of the human mind.* —

That without it, without this art, our entire education is nothing. Indeed I do not shrink, since once this sublime goddess, this guide of humanity is there, I do not shrink from calling her the *non plus ultra* of all education, on the basis that she warns and restrains us before every false step by her signs and explanations.

This art is no less pleasant and enticing. For in a few days it sets even a child of 15 years in the position of arguing against a person of 40–50 years about all things where the talk is not of printed law, of printed law which itself is the workshop of the devil whose evil informs all the ugly, boring detours of the court.

Since now, however, this sublime art of seeing the future does not have its residence in the hellish depths of dispute, it also indicates to us, in order to assure us, all the entrances and abysses of the same, all the voracious monsters which draw in the poor innocent victim under the deception of protecting them from their enemies, but with the true intention of sucking their blood right to the last drop.

Oh! You who, as the logician says, lives from the evil and misfortune of others, you gatekeepers, hounds and rats, you who wear all black clothes, come to me, now take only six hours of instruction in my sublime art of wisdom, and you will comprehend how this colour is the talisman of the devil who always induces to evil.

You will learn that we, without this science, exercise all virtues only like those animals which the learned show us to be either fearing being struck or hoping for a small reward. In fact, if you do not initiate yourself in this art of doing everything according to principle, then your virtue can only be based on the hope of a reward, or be supported by the fear of punishment if you refrain from it.

Yes, I dear to claim solemnly (in order not to explain here individually all the advantages which the science of this single art grants us on earth) that nobody before the hundreds and thousands of accidents which constantly threaten them has a place of refuge if they are not in possession of this prescient art, that nobody sleeps securely without it, indeed could wake securely.

But all that which we now say is certainly not the birth of a heated, crazy brain. Twenty pens could prove these truths, a hundred pens would avenge themselves against the ignorant who let themselves join in with the mocking of the great man, opposing the most sublime science of which they have no idea and no grasp.

Since now the learned interpreters of the Book of Thoth, who agree entirely with us, have shown by facts what I have now claimed, I now want immediately to lead the true lover and reverer to the theoretical and practical instruction of the third lesson in the Egyptian art of oracle. But before we come to that, we want to see beforehand whether we have not omitted or forgotten anything in the two previous lessons.

With the first time of placing the cards, you separate the entire Book of Thoth into three rows; which repeated three times gives the numbers 24, ... 11, 17, 26.

With the second time, after the cards were shuffled again, cut by the querent, and the entire Book gathered together again as one, you take from the top of the Book 17 cards, one after the after, and place them down. The oracle giver then looks at the 18th card which follows them, and the 78th as the last; without though letting the querent see these two cards. This leads us now to several remarks.

The false *art of laying the cards* has taken hold among people so much, and distanced the only true art of giving oracle from the Book of Thoth so that you do not come across any individual querent anymore who is not so curious to have a look at and inspect the cards as he cuts them.

Likewise you also have the superstition of paying attention to the day, and especially to carrying out the laying of cards on the first Friday of each month, as well as of drawing with the left hand. Indeed the superstition has even been introduced by the querent who believes in the conjuring of spirits of letting fall in the house of the soothsayer a pin, a piece of thread, or another small thing. But who does not see that this can have no connection at all with the events which they wish for the oracle giver to foretell.

That which is yet a birth of an ignorant gullibility consists of someone setting no proper bounds on their hope and trust. They always overstep the extreme; they believe and hope either for more than human knowledge allows, or they believe and hope instead for less than human knowledge can allow. And in both cases they are deceived and mistaken.

I thus advise you to withhold your judgement so that you never let their hope overstep the mark before you yourself are familiar with the matter and have heard the oracle. I say also, however, that the trust which is had in the unveiler of the future must not be greater than the salary which is given to him. For it would be wrong to expect an entirely complete picture of life circumstances when the querent has only paid the oracle giver for a small scrap of the same.

Most of the ignorant who, to their advantage, have considered it good to pay for soothsayers have wanted to draw the devil into their game — others again have followed the opposite, and considered the murmuring of prayers, psalms, Our Fathers, and Ave Marias before their oracle giving to be good and necessary.

You see from that how many have been seduced into considering something to be the philosophy of the oracle which is nothing of the sort at all, how many have thought to have found the true unveiler of the future either in a priest or in a conjuror of spirits.

Here is the true confession of my heart, which I would make if I were not bright, if I merely followed my experience and my heart.

I would learn the art of penetrating into the future, and dedicate myself to it because it is indispensable for the good and fortunate life — and because I believe that without this science it is impossible to escape only the twentieth part of the unfortunate events before which it protects and secures us. For only with this intention did the Egyptian wise men invent this sublime art, and we the script in order to write words.

If I had now learnt this art, at least as far as the second degree, then I would now continuing working in it for myself with the same industry as I practice daily for half an hour on the piano.

From time to time I would then have my instructor in the giving of oracles come in order to converse with him over the appreciation and the certainty of this art.

Here is now the place that I must recall that it is no less shameful to go to a true unveiler of the future as to go to a lawyer. But certainly you must here indulge the prejudices and the ignorance, and this all the more because many, always deceived by false fortune tellers and soothsayers, cannot convince themselves anymore, or only with difficulty, that actually a higher art, a higher sublime science is there than that which the common everyday fortune teller vaunts.

I repeat once more what I have already said frequently, that this mysterious science which has made me famous over all Europe, sometimes for good, sometimes for bad, according to whether you had true or false ideas of the matter, that this science, I say, will show once more in brighter light what nature, the mind, and all the sciences now teach us.

It is certainly not unknown to anyone how much Galileo was persecuted when he taught the motionlessness of the sun in the middle of the universe; what trouble Ramon Llull had in introducing the study of Oriental languages to Europe; and certainly finally everyone knows from experience what kind of resistance and contradiction is found everywhere for what one does not have enough mind to contrive and look into. But certainly, everyone is also convinced that, early or late, truth must win in the end. And this is also the only reward which I promise and hope for from my instruction and my efforts.

You indisputably recall what I have already explained, that namely the first procedure of placing the cards gave us the numbers 11, 17, 26, significant numbers with respect to the second and third time of placing the cards. But 11 is also with this third time of placing the cards more remarkable than any other number; since the 11 is also a number though which indicates human weakness; thus the third time of placing the cards cannot be as certain and dependable for the science of oracle giving as the second time. Likewise the fourth time of placing the cards is more certain and stronger than the third time, and the fifth time by contrast less strong than the fourth time. But all this which I am saying about the strength and weakness of the placing of cards in respect to the certainty of the oracle giving only concerns the speculative theory, or the philosophy of the Book of Thoth, and appertains only to the powers of comprehension of those who have arrived as far as the third degree of this science. This explanation can do nothing for those who have only arrived as far as the second degree, or probably even still stand in the first.

If we now thus have the Book of Thoth in our hand, then shuffle it, have it cut, and then put it together again.

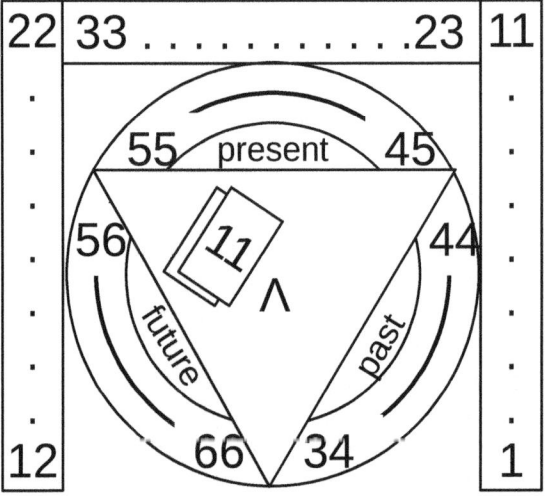

Now place the first card of the Book of Thoth at number 1 — and so on for the following cards up to number 11.

The 12th card which follows it at number 12 and thus the following cards again up to number 22.

The 23rd card at position 23 and the others across the transverse row up to number 33.

The 34th card at position 34 and the following cards in a circle through 44, 45, 55, 56, 66.

While you thus place the cards of the Book of Thoth in this order, you must still (if you are namely giving oracle to someone of the masculine gender) place card 1, if it should appear, in position Λ. However, you must, if you are unveiling the future from someone of the feminine gender, place card 8 in that position. Moreover the Λ, which stands in the centre of the circle, shall also indicate to you that all cards which form this circle must lie with the head towards Λ, but the legs towards the outside.

If card 1, which always represents the male querent (as card 8 represents the female querent), does not appear among the 66 placed cards, you must search for it among the 12 remaining cards. Then 11 cards still remain, for either only card 1, or card 8 must be in the middle in position Λ.

In this entire procedure of placing the cards, two things are especially noteworthy. The entire number of cards here amounts to 67, in this 11 is visible everywhere; secondly, the 7 points of the sphere, which are expressed and indicated by the 7 times 11[1]. And there are 8 parts, if you reckon the card which lies in the centre as a part. This form of card placing is generally named the *wheel of fortune*; but is better called *the revolution of the three periods of life*.

The cards which lie from 1 to 11 and from 34 to 44 indicate to us the past events, the occurrences of the *past*.

The cards which lie from 23 to 33 and from 45 to 55 show us the present, the occurrences of the *present*.

And the cards from 12 to 22 and from 56 to 66 unveil for us the events which will strike us in the *future*.

After you have now placed the 67 cards according to the prescribed order, pick up card 34 to your left and 1 to your right, and say this or that (which the cards show us) is past, has happened. You must every time take thus 2 cards, with the past, the present and the future.

The only thing which you must note with the cards which indicate the future is that you pick up 56 and 12 at the same time so that 66 and 22 coincide as the cards of the still later future. This procedure arise because 12 is put down earlier than 22.

When you have now explained everything you have found in these placed cards, and after you have collected them again, do not forget the 7 times 11 of this placing of cards, in that you are directed to it at the fourth time of placing, and must make it by the 7 or the 11.

---

1   [Tr.: i.e. the 6 placings of 11 plus the 11 remainder.]

But it is very good, since you have just made a very weak go in respect to the oracle giving, that you now make it a strong one, and that you take the number 7, since you already have had 11 as the image of weakness.

Indeed, since almost nothing at all shall remain hidden and veiled before you at the fourth time, you must already in this respect select the number 7 because it is the key to all things.

A lover of this science, however may perhaps note here that we have said elsewhere that 1, 3, 5 are the strong significant numbers, since we here in contrast accept and recognise 2, 4 before them.

Only you must note that I talked there of the numbers in themselves, and not, as now, of the number of times of placing the cards; that I spoke there of the numbers as causes, but not as now of the numbers as their simple characters. You must here merely see these numbers thus, 1, 3, 5, as something given of which you yourself form the cause, as with many other things. It is with our art just as in music, mathematics, and all other sciences when you are nothing but a mere copyist. You increase the useless appendages of science without knowing and practising them.

Finally, he who merely has practical knowledge and no genius for the science which always nourishes him must also by necessity take his refuge sooner or later in a confidence trick which exposes him to all shame.

Incidentally it is also certain, however, that the higher sciences are far easier than the common everyday science, simply because they, the more elevated they are, merely work through and for the mind.

It is just the same even with the fine arts, e.g. with painting. Although it has its difficulty, it is certainly accepted that it is far easier if you have a feeling for nature than if you have no sense for it.

Thus it is also far easier to see the truth than the lie; for the more something approaches nature, the easier it is for the human mind to comprehend it.

The art of giving oracle is in itself so simple that you must think it fitting for the most common child's mind, and so it also really is. But, like all sciences, it also always rises in stages to the more difficult, but without distancing itself from the power of comprehension of those who ask it.

In geometry the theorems likewise become more and more difficult the further you penetrate into its science.

The principles in the art of oracle giving are just as simple as true. You can never fail to recognise them. But, like every other art, ours also has its own spirit.

When two adepts argue somehow in this sublime art over a sentence, for example, over that which I will explain below, and which appears once in the instruction which I gave a member of the National Assembly — then they must proceed each time from first principles, and hold to them; but that they must also always pay attention to the innate spirit of those principles.

The sentence namely which I want to deliver, and the case which I experienced, deserve all the more the attention of all scholars, the more the correctness of language comes into play with it. Notwithstanding this last consideration, the spirit of our art must decide, however, as much as it follows all other sciences and arts.

You can really say that anyone who can give a correct explanation of the following three cards can also in a moment understand and learn the true principles of oracle giving.

34, displeasure. 44, future[1]. 31, gold.

According to the false principles, you read: gold in the future will cause you displeasure.

But according to the true principles, you read: you will give someone gold, and this one, this someone will cause you displeasure in the future.

According to the true principles and the genius of the art of seeing into the future, you must think of more numbers than the senses perceive, because this sentence, this instance really lays down actually six numbers for the mind, in this way: 1, 34, (44) Λ, 31, 1. This sign Λ indicates and signifies a person whose gender, age and circumstances are not defined here.

Thus, according to the true rules of the art, combined with the spirit of this science, the unveiler of the future must thus say by virtue of his signs and premonitions:

---

1   [Tr.: actually the reversed keyword of 44.]

You are willing to give someone gold. It is good that you are thinking about whether nothing may hinder you from it — I would not say that to you if instead of gold I merely saw money, and the reason why I would not ask you to is that gold already points to a large sum, but money merely to a few dollars, or at least to a smaller, tinier means — but you must think about it still more, because this one, this someone, will in the future 44 cause you displeasure 34, in relation to and because of the gold 31 which you want to now give him or lend to him; and this future will be there earlier, or come later than you surmise.

But if the order of the numbers were 34, 31, (44), then this would make a change with respect to the timing, and you would then have to say, according to the true principles and the spirit of our science:

$$1, 34, \Lambda, 31, (44) \ 1.$$

In the future you will give a person gold which will cause you displeasure which will drag on long into the future, and the loss of your gold is certain.

You will here surely think that in this way our art can hinder charitable support and magnanimity? — But are you noble-minded if you give away a large sum in relation to your means? — You act rashly and are careless.

That secondly our art could break up and cancel very advantageous negotiations where you draw interest? — But do the greatest negotiations in this way base themselves on greed? And can not sometimes the entire structure of speculation and benefiting collapse, and the lender and his means in the end be ruined entirely? —

Yes, the true sacred art of seeing into the future, this wisdom of life in the only true friend of humanity! Familiar with everything, she rises from the present and reveals to everyone all her secrets.

But with that now those who enjoy studying this sublime wise art are strengthened even more in their courage and their desire; thus I want now to say something about the change and about the various positions of the first three cards of the Book of Thoth[1]. I am convinced that you will not only hold onto what I describe here and what you read here, but rather that you yourself will take up the three cards before you and seek to place them differently so that they form different dialogues and sentences each time. There are, however, only six different placements possible, because the three 3 numbers, as is well-known to everyone, are only to be ordered differently six times.

3. 2. 1. The inquirer or querent will clarify undertakings, proposals, or an intention.

1. 3. 2. An explanation will apply to the intentions of the inquirer.

2. 1. 3. Someone makes proposals to the inquirer who will seek an explanation.

1. 2. 3. Proposals give the inquirer an explanation.

2. 3. 1. The inquirer will make proposals which will give someone an explanation.

3. 1. 2. Someone will give the inquirer an explanation which will lead him to make proposals.

This unique principle which we give here of correctly reading the meanings we find in the cards of the Book of Thoth is, as I believe, sufficient and confirmation enough. For the way of reading three cards shows us how we must read four cards and up to the greatest number 26 which can lie in a row.

But in order now to continue our third lesson to the end, I want now to mention a few things about the three steps of the science of giving the oracle.

We say that someone possesses the first degree of this art who firstly knows the physical course and procedure of the laying of cards five times, and who secondly also understands how to clothe in sentences and speech the meanings which each hieroglyph of the Book of Thoth offers them.

This first degree usually gives the newly entering apprentice in this art many pleasures; but as that which is merely pleasure never lasts long, so it also passes for the apprentice here into boredom and weariness — it would then have to be that he endeavours and understands to seek and to find in

---

1   [Tr.: 1 Male querent; 2 Explanation; 3 Intention (synonym: proposal).]

this first degree the true genuine copy and description of the connection of life incidents.

It is the same too with those who pretend to dedicate themselves entirely to this art. When they are limited by some cause only to this first degree of the art of seeing into the future, since moreover here the knowledge of giving oracle is very uncertain, their ignorance ensures that they soon abandon these studies, and choose another which puts chance and fortune in their hand straightaway.

Even for the querent it is very dangerous to fall into the hands of such a oracle giver who uses only trickery and deceit with his art. It is yet fortunate that these people reveal and characterise themselves straightaway by their thievish and deceitful faces.

If you only possess the first degree of this science, then you can also only be at most your own oracle giver, or for your friends and family. And moreover you can be this also merely in the cases where the actual art, science and knowledge of the Book of Thoth is dispensable.

But often with this first degree true information about the future can occur, even in fact because the oracle giver here has done nothing with the first degree other than merely stuck to the letters and words, and thus followed the common healthy understanding.

It happens far more often, however, that the oracle giver of the first degree can seek out and understand nothing at all from their glance at the cards, that they as it were find no doors to enter, no path on which they can walk, nor finally a door through which they could exit again.

Then it happens that the mere enthusiast of our art of the science of oracle giving considers it insufficient and false because the clumsy person who pretends to be a connoisseur, an adept of this art, takes his refuge only in false oracles, in lies in order to hide and conceal his ignorance.

The shiftiest of the ignorant confessors of this science need a ruse which the good-natured unsuspecting querent does not in general know.

They seek namely to affect the enthusiasm of the great wise philosophers, as did also the sibyls, the unholy godless priests, and similar charlatans as well. They act as if they fall into a deep silence, which with the true philosophers is an effect of their great astonishment, contemplation and wisdom, and then leap up, the ignoramuses! — with the most ridiculous gestures.

The second degree of oracle giving actually gives us a proper idea of this art, and it is then very rare if you have gotten that far that you should merely remain an enthusiast or mediocre connoisseur of it. This is the same case with all who spend time with sciences and arts — they always find more taste for it, the more they advance in it.

With this second degree, as also with the third, you must not, however, neglect and forget the first physical rules of the first degree — you must just add to it the spirit of the science, and also raise yourself at the same time to other supernatural principles, and finally to the divine.

There you must begin to pass judgement yourself in this art. The geometer describes, however, on three given points, figures and circles, the skilled master builder constructs over already present foundations castles and palaces — so too must the sublime unveiler of the future himself, after the second degree, bring about constructions, forms and figures in the spirit of the art.

The first degree in the art of giving oracle is like a quick-learning child who repeats back everything to his teacher. The second degree is a grown youth who thinks about the wise instruction of his teacher, sees the reasons, familiarises himself with the spirit of his science, its art, and the wisdom which was recorded by the first Egyptians in the Book of Thoth.

As far as the third degree of our sublime art is concerned, the possessor is as in all other arts and sciences the now completely cultivated person who works firmly and steadfastly according to the eternal principles of the art, thus serves it so happily that, if it were music, connoisseurs and fans of it, indeed even all unfeeling humans would cry out at once, what melody, what harmony! What truth in this divine art! —

The oracle giver who understands the third degree is a rare phenomenon; but he is a Raphael, a Poussin, a Le Sueur[1] in

---

1   [Tr.: Raffaello Sanzio da Urbino (1483–1520), Italian painter and architect; Nicolas Poussin (1594–1665), French painter; and Jean-

relation to it. Up to this moment I know of almost none publicly. Few people have the fortune of reaching as far as the
level of the hermetic philosophy! —[1]

The fourth time of placing cards, to which we now come,
helps us penetrate into the deepest mysteries of the past,
present and future, if they namely lie in the order of human
things, and if God has not expressly commanded that they remain veiled and hidden. However, the unveiling of things,
with which our science occupies itself, is based on order and
on human nature, and not forbidden by the will of the highest
as a proud revolt against the laws of nature. Who can surely
be so blind, so limited; who should not find that it has been
preannounced by the highest himself more than a thousand
times?

For nature could surely point us to the art of unveiling the
future more distinctly, more clearly than by giving us the
weapon in our hands with which we should protect and de-
fend ourselves against the events of live?

When you have now again taken up the cards which you
had set down for the third time, shuffled them, and have had
them cut — then ask yourself now (if you namely want to unveil your events yourself), or the one to whom you should give
the oracle, what has not occurred in the three times of placing
the cards? What is it that you or he would like to know? —
And over that you must then thus place the cards for the
fourth time, and query the Book of Thoth. E.g.: if you desire
to know: Shall I undertake this? — Will I receive a letter? —
Will I obtain money? — Spend money? Deal with money? In
short, just what you want the Book of Thoth to answer and
unveil for you.

I must once more note that the fourth time of placing the
cards is the strongest of all five, and that nothing here can remain veiled which God has not expressly kept for himself.

François Le Sueur (1760–1837), French composer.]

1 [Tr.: the French edition consulted finished the third lesson here with
   the comment: "Too overloaded with occupations, I cannot now give
   what is missing between page 72 and 145". What follows to the end of
   the section is actually the operative part of the fourth lesson from the
   French edition, which bears no resemblance to the fourth lesson of the
   German translation, which concerns dream interpretation.]

But before I continue, I must say to all those who want to become masters in this science that it is very essential that they forget nothing at all of what they have found with the previous times of placing the cards. For only by a good faithful memory, or if you have written everything down, can you after the terminal fifth time of placing the cards list in an orderly and observant manner the temporal sequence of all the person's events from their birth to the last moment of their death, and form a register of their life.

The questions to which you expect an answer from the Book of Thoth must be clear and comprehensible; not mysteriously clothed, not so that they contain anything ambiguous or uncertain.

The unveiler of the future must in particular pay special attention to the question and be attentive if he has not yet gotten to know the querent from the Book of Thoth as an upright good person; also when the first three times of placing the cards have not occurred yet. But the true oracle givers will themselves observe all this easily, and all the other traps which could be set as snares for them by evil persons.

When the cards are thus shuffled, cut and placed together as one again; then you put the questions, and for each question you draw 7 cards.

If the first 7 cards indicate nothing, answer nothing to the question, then you draw 7 others; and if these again say nothing, 7 cards once more for the third time.[1]

This fourth time of placing the cards is amongst everything the hardest because the answer to the question does not expose itself here at once and so quickly for reading off.

If, for example, the question is whether you will receive money, letters, or something else altogether, then you must, in order to give and to know the time when this will happen (if in fact nothing about this time is indicated in the 7 cards), look at the first, second and third 7 cards in order to find this

---

1   [Tr.: here in the French edition, Etteilla refers the reader to page 30, paragraph 2 of his book *Manière de se récréer avec le jeu de cartes nommées tarots: pour servir de troisième cahier a cet ouvrage* (1783), where he suggests that if the repetitions find nothing, the querent should be urged to pray, change their conduct, and return in a few days.]

and give oracle about it. In this case, the time is indicated, reveals itself through one of the three rules which you accepted before you undertook to find the answers in the cards.

Were the magic oracle giver to possess all possible knowledge, then he would not at all need more than 7 cards to answer a question. At least it is certain that the topmost of the Egyptian priests never had need for more than 7 cards to decide a question.

It is also this by which you can recognise the true unveiler of the future from the false or mediocre one.

Ha! Who now can, however, without the divine friend, the goddess who teaches us to look into the future, make a thorough examination of our life, who can, I say, without her show with certainty the cliffs onto which we will run like errant ships on the waves of the sea, the cliffs upon which our little ship will break and sink into the stormy abyss? — Can human cleverness do it? — No, it cannot, it leads us surely still more astray into the deceptive swamps of faint, distantly shining lights, the more we want to avoid and escape them. — Only it is the divine power which resides in the temples of antiquity, the art which the old Egyptians teach us, and which I teach you again — the art of the mind, the medicine of the heart, and the consoling balm of humanity!

Fourth Lesson[1]

Fourth drawing of the Book of Thoth, indicating and explaining truly all dreams and all premonitions according to the doctrine of the old Egyptians

Even dreams come from God — — when the soul, free, un-shackled from the body, wings its way from this prison, it glides over the acts of life which have long since fallen into the stream of time; but also it also glides over acts which are yet to come, which appear in the series of things, and shall be done by the living machine. Who can deny the soul the capab-ility of foreseeing? We have proven above that it is possible, indeed necessary according to the Book of Thoth. Who can deprive the soul, but still more in the night where it sinks more calmly into itself and is not disturbed by the intrusion of the world of sensation, who can deprive you there, I say, of the feeling of seeing into the future, of making out what you will encounter, or the bodies which they inhabit will meet? No, nobody can do this — for even God makes use of dreams to say to people, indeed often to the entire human race, through them what sort of times would come, and what he wanted them to do in those times. But none of all the printed works over dreams, premonitions and apparitions reaches and touches the thousandth part of that which strikes us daily. It is the Book of Thoth alone which stretches over everything, and nothing of all that which we encounter is left unexplained.

---

1   [Tr.: this fourth lesson may correspond to the missing fifth or sixth les-sons of the original French edition – only four out of six planned les-sons were included in the original.]

We thus offer to all who are eager for knowledge the hidden science of how the old Egyptians explained dreams and premonitions — a science to whose instruction we now continue without hesitation.

In order to explain premonitions, dreams and apparitions, and to understand what we will say about them, you must, however, necessarily have the Book of Thoth in hand.

The cards of this Book must also be titled according to the manner of the Egyptians; for this Book was really, as we have proven elsewhere, the book of oracle for this people.

As Joseph said to the prisoners, "*Tell* me your *dreams which you have had*", those who have had such a dream or premonition must also put it down and write it up.

The wise explainer, however, must be instructed as much as possible as to the gender, the age, the condition and the entire circumstances of the person who has had the dream. But should the circumstances and considerations be such that the person wishes to be unknown and not to be named, then the explainer of the dream must first take his refuge in the Book of Thoth and the science of knowing absent things, which certainly makes his work more difficult. The one who has had the dream, however, can specify general features without revealing their identity and compromising themselves — so that the explainer can work all the more easily and certainly.

When now, as said above, the dream, the premonition or the apparition is to be drawn up as clearly and simply as possible in writing, then the explainer or the one eager for knowledge must themselves compose the dream, for example, in an orderly story according to the cards. The only difficulty here, if it can be called that, is that the story with the cards is made so clearly and comprehensibly that even the child can read it to them in and from the cards, and understand and explain it according to the meanings which the cards have.

But it is also unnecessary that you write down the dream on paper beforehand if you can depict and describe it straightaway through the cards — it is just as unnecessary that you write the meaning of each card on them if you understand them yourself and can recite them by heart. In a single hour you can learn to explain all possible dreams just as you can in about six hours learn the art of giving oracle from the Book of Thoth and unveiling the future.

We have already said that you must have the Book of Thoth before you, and that the cards of it must also be numbered. If you thus have this book before you, then you must (in order to give the example of a dream here which I will explain below) place the cards before you in a single row in order as per the following numbers: the 21 to the left hand of the explainer, and the 28 to his right. But the numbers enclosed in the parentheses must be placed down so that they are not seen[1]: 21, 1, 34, 5, (24) 66, 57, (49) 43, 13, 20, 74, 22, 38, 73, (39) 8, 48, (58) 67, 32, 68, 28.

If the cards are not placed as the numbers here indicate, then it is impossible for the explainer to be able to comprehend and see the cards as all possible dreams, premonitions, apparitions are contained in the Book of Thoth; secondly it is also impossible that he can explain the dream properly and truly. But when the dream or the premonition is described and placed exactly through the cards, then the explanation must certainly astonish and convert the most disbelieving. Here is the dream which a lady had, and which she has allowed us to make known publicly with its explanation.

Dream

I dreamt as if I were in the *countryside* in a *house* where there was *company*. A *young brown man* made a *declaration of love* to me there which *flattered* me so that I wanted to accept him as *lover* when just then *a man entered* who was far superior in rank and means to the former.

This second arrival offered me his *means* and the gift of his hand, that is, he wanted to *marry me*. Then now gave me the *idea* of *changing* my decision — but made me keep the *hope* of being *useful* to the first man. But my changed decision brought about that he *fell out* and broke with me, and as it appeared to me, started a *jour-*

---

1   [Tr.: the ensuing description suggests that this indicates they take their reversed meaning. Note also that they are read right to left.]

ney out of annoyance and went away. This now gave me much *sorrow* so that I imagined that he who was now travelling away was really my *friend*; the man by contrast who I had preferred and chosen was, if he wanted to make me straightaway into a great rich lady, the enemy of my friend; and that hence my true real friend would heap on me now hard reproaches, as I deserved them. This all caused me to suddenly wake up so that I was *morose* all day and did not let anybody see me.

I beg you, my lord, to now explain this dream to me exactly and according to the truth so that I can either enjoy in advance the pleasure which it foretells for me, or that I can brace myself for the bad things which it indicates.

If you place the cards before yourself as was indicated above, then you will straightaway perceive two things in particular:

1. that even a child of five or six years could interpret this dream;
2. that it is impossible that the explainer could add anything more than the dream really indicates.

In addition, you see that there is no single book which contains all possible dreams, premonitions and apparitions, and that also not once is a book found which gives us a continuing entire explanation as we do and teach. It always says there merely: *to dream of a man* signifies *honour for a woman*; *to dream of a woman* signifies *society for a man and intention for a woman*. This is surely also true, but nevertheless it is no continuing explanation of a dream as we give them. Finally too, all known books over dreams have nothing similar in the manner of their interpretation with that of the Egyptians, nor with that which served *Joseph* to explain the dreams to the *Pharaoh*.

Explanation of the Above Dream

Madame, since the unease in which the dream put you has moved you to the step of taking your refuge in the science in which the first most sublime wise men of all peoples were initiated and known as great — I thus take every freedom to again give you the ease which you have lost, and to unveil the truth to you purely and truly.

The explainer picks up two cards at once each time[1].

28. 21. You will get into an *argument*, fall into disagreement in the *countryside*.

68. 1. Your *friend* will come and seek *entrance* to your house.

32. 34. You will give the opportunity in *company* for *annoyance*.

67. 5. On a *journey*, you will find a young *brown man* who will be thought by you to be the one whom you saw in the dream.

(58. 24.) You will *break off* something by an *explanation*.

48. 66. *Benefit* of the *love* signifies harmony, friendship, union as the goal of your present affair.

8. 57. Someone has *intentions* for *you*, or hopes from you for an obliging service.

(39. 49.) One of the objects who *flatters* you most will *change*, but this seems to be to your advantage.

72. 34. You constantly have your *thoughts* on the one who *loves* you.

38. 13. A *wedding happens*. Since the dream has to much order than that it should not fit entirely to you, you will not hesitate to marry your *friend*. And if you wish to know the time of the wedding, then I must say to you that it will happen by itself within 53 days and a few hours[2].

22. 20. You will seek to make a part of your *fortune* with a *great man*. Here I can give you the assurance, according to the naturally true interpretation of the dream, that you will go well here.

74. You expect a *gift* which you will not receive though.

***

---

1 [Tr.: note that the cards are paired from opposite ends of the row.]

2 When you want to know the time something will happen, as, for example, the wedding, then you must multiply the number 13 (the card which signifies marriage) with the second one after it in the upper row, which is 49, 13 x 49 = 637. Then you must divide the 637 by 12 (as the number of hours in the day [sic]), and so arrive at 53 days and a remainder of 1. This 1 = 24 hours, you divide again by 12, and thus derive 2 hours.

If you have according to the Book of Thoth made the sublime title of a high explainer of dreams your own, and attained it, which can happen in a short time, after two to three days work and industrious study, then you are then in a position, with the help of that Book which contains the science of the entire universe, to explain and truly interpret all possible dreams and apparitions.

Appendix: Key Words and Synonyms

No.	Upright	Reversed
0/78	**Foolishness:**[1] Insanity, extravagance, insanity, bewilderment. Drunkenness, delirium, hot fever, frenzy, rage, fury, transport. Enthusiasm. Blindly, ignorantly. Fool, irreconcilable, innocent, simple, silly.	**Foolishness:** Imbecility, ineptitude, insouciance, stupidity, imprudence, negligence, absence, distraction. Apathy, fainting, annihilation, sleep, nothing, nullity, void, empty, futile.
1	**Etteilla or the male querent** (Aries): God almighty, eternal, most high, the trinity, supreme being; the spirit of God, the central spirit, chaos, glory; the immortal man; the male querent. Thought, meditation, contemplation, reflection, contention of spirit, mental research.	**The male querent:** Philosopher, philosophical, philosophically, to philosophize. Wise, wisdom, wisely.

---

1   [Tr.: keywords and astrological signs, etc. are from the German edition, whereas the synonyms are a rough translation from *Dictionnaire synonymique du livre de Thot* (1791), published by Etteilla's son, his student Claude Hugand, and Samson.]

No.	Upright	Reversed
2	**Explanation** – 2nd element, 1st day of creation (Taurus): Information, unraveling, development, instruction, opening, analysis, discovery, interpretation, revelation, clarity: elucidation, light, radiation, glory, fire, sun, temple of heat. Eternal bulwark; heaven and earth, glorification.	**Fire**: Heat. Clarification; spark, ray of light, gleam, flame, conflagration, burn, ardour. Fire of love, flame, passion, ignite, enflame. Meteors; lightning, thunder, storm, electricity, St Elmo's fire, magnetism; outer fire, inner fire, central fire, magnet, sulphur, philosophical fire, salamander. Fire, dissension, mental discord; venting anger; making fire & flame, bone of contention. Heat, cook: heating, inflammation.
3	**Intention** – 1st element, 3rd day of creation (Gemini): Purpose, resolution, will; speech, discourse, reasoning: to speak, to discourse, to chatter, to cause. Babble, gossip, gossip, slander, slander, defamation. The moon.	**Water**: Fluidity, wetness, ablution: dew, pouring rain, deluge, flood; sea, river, torrent, stream, fountain, source, lake, marsh, sheet of water, pond, waterfall, waves, ebb and flow; humidity, vapour, impregnated, smoke, mercury, catholic water, mercurial water, philosophical water, merfolk, emanation, frost, snow, ice, exhalation, evaporation. Secrecy, discretion. Silence; murmur, circumspection.

No.	Upright	Reversed
4	**Robbery** – 3rd element, 2nd day of creation (Cancer): Auditing, development, sorting, analysis, separation; unravel, deepen, disentangle. To take away, to deprive, to abduct, to despoil, to violate, to profane, to infringe; offering, violence. Deprivation, kidnapping, abduction, theft, larceny, trickery, fraud, swindle, infidelity.	**Air:** Wind, hurricane, atmosphere, climate, country, native air, dryness, drought. Sky, stars, birds, subtle, volatility. Tone, manner, pace, turn, appearance, semblance, resemblance, similarity, pretense, pretense, dissimulation, pretense, feign, hypocrisy. Song, music, tone, sound, acoustics: aerial, sylph. Idle talk, light talk, vague words. Melody. Song, supposition.
5	**Journey** – 4th element, 6th day of creation (Leo): Route, displacement, pilgrimage, peregrination, marches, steps, visits, races, incursions, emigration, transmigration, elopement, flight, rout, rotation, circulation. To disorient, confuse, disconcert, separate the dogs.	**Earth:** Cold, thick, material, mud, silt, silt, raw material, sulfur and mercury, leaf mould, virgin earth, Adamic earth, salt of the wise, female gnome. World; state, kingdom, empire, land, buildings, effects, possessions, rural property, prairies, meadows, orchards, fields, vines: reptiles. Country, regions, places, site, local, landscape, aspect, permanence, constancy, perseverance, tranquility, stagnation, inertia, shores, beach, sides, rock, reef; plain, mountain, hill, valley. Animals, beasts; brutes, quadrupeds.

No.	Upright	Reversed
6	**Night** (Virgo): Darkness, obscurity; nocturnal; mystery, secret, mask, hidden, unknown, clandestine, occult, eclipse, veil, emblem, figure, image, parable, allegory, mystical meaning, veiled remarks, mysterious words, obscure speeches; occult sciences. Leading the deaf, dark steps, clandestine actions, in secret, unreason, blindness, confuse, cover, envelop; forget, oblivion.	**Day**: Clarity, light, radiance, splendor, illumination, manifestation, evidence, truth. Clear, vivid, bright, enlighten, illuminate, give birth, bring to light, print, hatch; pierce. Enlighten, acquire knowledge. Public joys, fireworks. Zodiac.
7	**Support** – 5th day of creation (Libra): Support, prop, column; base, foundation; principle, reason, cause, future. Fixity; assurance, persuasion, conviction, sleuthing, security, certainty, confidence; aid.	**Increase**: Defence, assistance, aid, succour, influence, benevolence, charity, humanity, goodness, commiseration, pity, compassion, authorisation.
8	**Etteilla** – day of rest (Scorpio): Nature. Repose, tranquility, retreat, private life, seclusion, solitary life, life of the hermit, religious life, Orphic life; repose of the old men, temple of heat. Silence, taciturnity.	**The female querent**: Imitation, the Garden of Eden, effervescence, bubbling, fermentation, leaven; acidity.
9	**Justice** (Sagittarius): Equity, probity, uprightness, right, rectitude, reason; court, execution, justice. Thoth, or the Book of Thoth.	**Government**: Legislation, legislator; laws, decrees, codes, ordinance, statutes, precepts, command, domination; institution, conflict, temperament, complexion, natural laws, moral laws, religious laws, civil laws, political laws. The law of nations, public law, martial law.

No.	Upright	Reversed
10	**Moderation** (Capricorn): Moderation, difference, continence, abstinence, patience, calm, sobriety, frugality, chastity. Alleviation, consideration, accommodation, confederation. Reconciliation; conciliation, tempering of musical notes; temperature of air: climate. Thoth or the Book of Thoth.	**Spirituality**: Minister, priest, priesthood; clergy, church, council, synod, religion, sects.
11	**The strong** (Aquarius): Advantage through strength. Moral strength, greatness of soul, magnanimity, heroism, courage, perseverance, constancy. Power, empire , ascending. Spiritual or moral work. Patience, resignation. Domination. Thoth or the Book of Thoth.	**The sovereign**: Kingdom, empire, republic, state, government , administration. Reign, despotism, sovereignty, authority, command, supreme power, absolute power, powerful citizen, people, nation. King, emperor, general, commander,captain, superior leader, governor, dominator, motor, regulator, conservator, protector. Weakness, defectiveness, discrepancy.
12	**Cleverness** (Pisces): Wisdom, reserve, circumspection, restraint, discernment; foresight, prediction, prognosis, divination, prophecy, horoscope. Thoth or the Book of Thoth.	**The people**: Nation, legislator, sovereign, political corps, population, generation.
13	**Marriage** (sign of death of 14): Alliance, reunion, bond, marriage: vow, leaven; intimacy, bonding; trimming, joining, conjunction, copulation, coupling, chain, slavery, embarrassment, captivity, servitude.	**Union**: Society, acquaintance, concubinage, adultery, incest. Alloy, mixture, amalgam. Peace, concord, agreement, harmony, good intelligence, reconciliation.

No.	Upright	Reversed
14	**Major force** (sign of death of 15): Force, human force, extraordinary powers, capabilities, physical force, virtue, violent impulse, force of genius. Ravages, violence, coercion, vehemence, firmness, force of spirit. Manual or physical labour.	**Minor force**: Nimbleness, weakness, pettiness, tenderness, diminishment, failing, fainting. Abatement, depression, languor. Subsidence. Sin, offence, sacrilege.
15	**Sickness** (sign of death of 16): Physical, spiritual, or soul's malady. Wrong state of health or affairs: derangement. Infirmity, pain, poison, epidemic, plague, gangrene. Anguish, agony. Wrong, displeasure, damage, mishap, misfortune, disaster. Health, salubrity, stoutness. Catechism. Earthquake.	**Sickness**: Indisposition, unpleasantness, headache, heartache, lethargy, unfortunate position, disgrace, inconvenience, unease, melancholy, affliction, medicine, remedy. Charlatan, empirical, wise man.
16	**Judgement** (sign of death of 17): Opinion. Judgment of true, good, false, just. Discernment, intelligence, conception, reason, understanding, good judgment, fair spirit, genius. Reasoning, comparison, deliberation, view, thought; opinion, feeling, last judgment; biblical flood.	**Judgement**: Arrest, decree, deliberation, decision, arbitration, pacification. Poor judgment, weak spirit. Pusillanimity. Insanity. Injustice, simplicity, stupidity.
17	**Mortality** (sign of death of 13): Death, last breath, end, extinction, annihilation, destruction, attack, murder, assassination, homicide, suicide, regicide, massacre, carnage, butchery, slaughter, poisoning. Alteration, decay, corruption, putrefaction.	**Nothing** (sign of death of 13): Inertia, sleep, paralysis, lethargy, fainting, petrification, negation, nullity, annulment, to paralyse, to petrify, to ruin, to put to sleep, somnambulism.

No.	Upright	Reversed
18	**Libeller, Forger**: Foolish, hypocritical, fanatic, imposter, suborner, corruptor. Betrayal, hypocrisy, fanaticism, disguise, dissimulation, ruse, deceit, imposture.	**Libeller**: Hermit, anchorite, solitary, sleepwalker, hidden, concealed, disguise, politic, end; ruse.
19	**Misfortune**: Indigence, famine, poverty, distress, calamity, adversity, mishap, misfortune, chagrin, pain, torment, grief, affliction, inconvenience. Punishment, punishment of God, correction, chastisement. Reverse, disgrace, severity, rigidity, rigour.	**Prison**: Imprisonment, detention, arrest, captivity, slavery, tyranny, despotism, yoke, chains, prison cell. House of God, servitude, subjection.
20	**Fortune**: Happiness, felicity, amelioration, improvement, benediction, prosperity. Property, riches, benefits, graces, favours. Fate, destiny, adventure, good fortune.	**Growth, Increase**: Increase, aggrandisement, abundance. Growth, vegetation, production.
21	**Discord**: Troubles, riots, agitation, insurrection, revolt, sedition, faction, conspiracy, rebellion, defection. War, battle, conflict, combat, duel. Pride, vanity, faux glory, pomp, ostentation, audacity, temerity. Violence, disorder, anger, injury, outrage, presumption, vengeance.	**Discord, Argument**: Noise, din, dispute, quarrel, difference, contest, harassment, argumentation, debate.
22	**Man of the countryside** (king of sceptres): Honest man, conscience, probity. Rustic, villager, peasant, labourer, cultivator: agriculture.	**Good, serious man**: Indulgent, severity, leniency, complacency, tolerance, condescension.

No.	Upright	Reversed
23	**Woman of the countryside** (queen of sceptres): Household, domestic economy, honest woman, decency, civility, politeness, mildness. Virtue, honour, chastity.	**Beautiful, good woman**: Beauty, excellence: obliging, unofficial, helpful. Kind deed, service, alms, obligation.
24	**Departure** (knight of sceptres): To part. Journey, distance, absence, abandon, change, flight, desertion, migration. Transposition, translation, transplantation, transmutation. Evasion.	**Separation, quarrel, hate**: Falling out, rupture, dissension, division, separation. Faction, party. Quarrel, wrangle. Break, fracture. Discontinuation, interruption.
25	**Stranger** (knave of sceptres): Strange, uncommon, unusual, unknown, unprecedented, extraordinary, surprising, admirable, marvellous, prodigy, miracle. Episode, digression. Anonymity.	**News, novelty**: Announcement, instruction, opinion, warning, admonition, anecdotes, chronicle, history; tales, fables. Ideas, education.
26	**Female betrayer** (10 sceptres): Cunning, perfidy, deceit, ruse, surprise, disguise, dissimulation, hypocrisy; prevarication, duplicity, disloyalty, darkness, scoundrel, deceitful. Conspiracy. Impostor.	**Obstacle**: Unforeseen difficulty; bar, hindrance, embarrassment, opposition, upset, difficulty, pain, travail, inconvenience, objection, chicane, reclamation, pitfall. Hurdle, entrenchment, redoubt, fortification.
27	**Delay** (9 sceptres): Delay, adjournment, dismissal, suspension, removal, extension, slowness, slowing down.	**Crosspiece**: Obstacle, unforeseen difficulty, upset, disadvantage, adversity, pain, misfortune, mishap, calamity.

No.	Upright	Reversed
28	**Country life** (8 sceptres): Agriculture, cultivation, plough-ing, real estate, buildings, farm, tenant farm, garden, orchard, meadow, wood, grove, shade, pleasure, diversions, amuse-ment, pastimes, recreation, cel-ebration. Peace, calm, tranquil-ity, innocence. Village life, forest, valley, mountain, barn. War campaign.	**Inner unease:** Dissension, regrets, remorse, re-pentance, inner agitation. Irresol-ution, uncertainty, indecision. In-conceivable, incomprehensible. Doubt, scruples, timid con-science.
29	**Speaking** (7 sceptres): Discourse, discussion, sym-posium, conversation, disserta-tion, deliberation. Speech, pro-nunciation, grammar, dictionary, language, idiom, jargon, patois. Negotiation, market, exchange, measure, commerce, traffic, cor-respondence. Dialect, state-ments, to hurl, to confer, to gos-sip; to cause, to devise; prattle, chatter.	**Indecisive:** Irresolution, uncertainty, per-plexity; fickleness, looseness, variation, variety, diversity. Hes-itation. To stagger, to vacillate, versatility.
30	**Domestic** (6 sceptres): Servant, valet, lackey, mercen-ary, subordinate, slave; mail, concierge, message, announce-ment, commission. Household. Servitude.	**Expectation:** Hope, expectation, trust, foresight, fear, apprehension.
31	**Gold** (5 sceptres): Riches, opulence, magnificence, sumptuousness, éclat, luxury; abundance, goods; physical, philosophical or moral sun.	**Process, contradiction:** Litigation, difference, wrangle, contestation, dispute, upset, dis-cussion, chicanery, harassment; contradiction, inconsistency.

No.	Upright	Reversed
32	**Society** (4 sceptres): Association, assembly, liaison, federation, confederation, church: gathering, multitude, mob, crowd; troupe, band, company, cohort, army, convocation, accompaniment, mixture, alloy, amalgam.	**Happy progress**: Augmentation, growth, advancement, success; happiness, felicity, beauty, embellishment.
33	**Undertaking** (3 sceptres): To embark on, commence; usurp, to take over, audacity, temerity, boldness, impudence. Enterprising, hardy. Business, embarrassed, to disconcert. Crippled.	**Pains coming to an end**: End, cessation, discontinuation; interruption of mishap, of torture, of pain, of travail.
34	**Displeasure** (2 sceptres): Sadness, affliction, displeasure, grief, desolation, mortification, mood, falling out, melancholy, fumes, dark thoughts.	**Surprise**: Deceit, misrepresentation, trickery, mistake; trouble, emotion, fear, terror, dread, horror; consternation, surprise, admiration, rapture. Alarm. Marvel, phenomenon, miracle.
35	**Falling down** (1 baton): Cascade, decadence, decline, deterioration, reduction, dissipation, bankruptcy, ruin, destruction, demolition damage, ravage. Mistake, error. Despondency, depression, discouragement. Perdition, reflection, chasm, precipice. To perish, to fall, to demean oneself, to infringe. Depth.	**Birth**: Nativity, origin, creation; source, commencement, principle, primacy, the first. Extraction, race, family, house, line, posterity, occasion, cause, reason, premier, beginnings.

No.	Upright	Reversed
36	**Blond man** (king of cups): Honest man; probity, equity; arts, sciences.	**Man in place**: Man of distinguished rank; honest man, dishonest man. Mischievousness, exaction, pillage, misappropriation, injustice, waste, dilapidation. Thief, rascal, brigand.
37	**Blond woman** (queen of cups): Honest woman; virtue, wisdom, honesty.	**Woman in place**: Woman of distinguished rank. Honest woman, dishonest woman; vice, dishonesty, depravation, disorder, corruption; scandal.
38	**Arrival** (knight of cups): Approach, access, welcome, rapprochement, conformity; advent, reunion, approximation, incidental, affluence, comparison.	**Deception, guile**: Deceit, villainy, misrepresentation, ruse, artifice, finesse, dexterity, suppleness, trickery, swindle, subtlety, irregularity. Darkness.
39	**Blond boy** (knave of cups): Studious. Study, application, travail, reflection, observation, consideration, meditation, contemplation, occupation, job, profession, employ.	**Inclination, tendency**: Direction, propensity, inclination, attraction, taste, sympathy, passion, affection, attachment, amity. Heart, craving, desire, attraction, engagement, seduction, invitation, agreement; flattery, wheedling, toadying, adulation, eulogy, praise. Courtesan. To coax, to tempt. Sirens' song.
40	**City** (10 cups): Town; homeland, country, borough, village, place, site, residence, habitation. Citizen.	**Disfavour**: Indignation, agitation, irritation, anger, fury, violence, frenzy, rage, hatred, aversion, animadversion, animosity, antipathy, resentment, vengeance. Danger, risk, peril. Injury, affront, outrage, blasphemy, storm, tempest, whirlwind. Cruelty, inhumanity, atrocity, enormity.

No.	Upright	Reversed
41	**Victory** (9 cups): Success, advantage, gain. Pomp, triumph, trophy, majesty, spectacle, device, gear.	**Sincerity**: Verity, reality, loyalty, frankness, ingenuousness, naivety. Liberty, licence, familiarity, boldness, ease, disturbance.
42	**Blond girl** (8 cups): Honest girl, modest girl, honour, modesty, shame, restraint, timidity, fear, apprehension. Mildness.	**Satisfaction**: Pleasure, happiness, contentment, gaiety, joy, rejoicing, entertainment; festival, Sunday. Excuse, reparation, exculpation. Public joy, spectacle, device, affectation, preparation, disposition.
43	**Thought** (7 cups): Soul, spirit, intelligence, idea, memory, imagination, understanding, conception, meditation, contemplation; reflection, deliberation, opinion, sentiment.	**Proposal**: Design, intention, desire, will, resolution, determination, premeditation.
44	**Past** (6 cups): Preterite, past prime, faded, withered. Ancient, previously, before, formerly, in olden days; old age, decrepitude, antique.	**Future**: Afterwards, later, subsequently. Regeneration, resurrection. Reproduction, renewal, reiteration.
45	**Inheritance** (5 cups): Succession, legacy, gift, donation, dowry, endowment, legitimate, patrimony, transmission, testament, tradition, revelation, cabal.	**Relations**: Consanguinity, blood, family, forefathers, ancestors, father, mother, brother, sister, uncle, aunt, cousin, Adam and Eve; filiation, extraction, race, line; alliance, affinity, contacts, rapport, liaison.

No.	Upright	Reversed
46	**Long while** (4 cups): Displeasure, discontentment; disgust, aversion, enmity, hate, horror; anxiety, spiritual pain, light grief, affliction. Tiresome, detrimental, unpleasant; grievous, depressing.	**New acquaintance**: New instruction, new information, new light, new intelligence, new clarification. Sign, indication, conjecture, augur, presage, presentiment, prognosis, oracle, prediction, prophesy, divination. Novelty.
47	**Success** (3 cups): Happy ending, victory. Recovery, cure, relief. Accomplishment, perfection.	**Expedition**: Dispatch, execution, achievement, ending, conclusion, termination.
48	**Love** (2 cups): Passion, inclination, sympathy, appeal, propensity, amity, benevolence, affection, attachment, taste, liaison, gallantry, attraction, affinity.	**Yearning**: Wish, vow, will, craving, desire, cupidity, lust, jealousy, passion, illusion, appetite.
49	**Banquet** (1 cup): Repast, feast, gala, culinary delight; nourishment, food, nutrition; conviviality, service. Invitation, prayer, supplication, convocation, invocation. Host, hotel, inn, hostel, cabaret, cork, tavern. Abundance, fertility, production, solidity, stability, steadiness, constancy, perseverance, continuation, life, next course, diligence, persistence, obstinacy, firmness, courage, tableau, painting, image, hieroglyph, description. Shelf, wallet, office, secretary; picnic, bronze table, marble table, law; catalogue, table of contents of the Book of Thoth. Garden table, sounding board.	**Change**: Mutation, permutation, transmutation, alternation, vicissitude, variety, variation, inconstancy, mildness; exchange, barter, purchase, sale, progress, treaty, convention. Metamorphose, diversity, versatility, reversal, distressing, revolution, reversion, translation, interpretation.

No.	Upright	Reversed
50	**Man of standing**: Man of law, judge, counsellor, senator, man of affairs, practitioner, advocate, prosecutor, doctor; jurist; jurisprudence. Litigant, legal expert.	**Evil man**: Bad intentions, malice, perversity, treachery, crime, cruelty, inhumanity, atrocity.
51	**Widowhood**: Period before a widow can remarry, privation, absence, famine, sterility. Poverty, indigence.	**Evil woman**: Malignancy, malice, deceit, finesse, artifice, mischievousness, bigotry, prudery, hypocrisy.
52	**Military**: Swordsman, man at arms, fencing master, hired killer. Hunter. Officer, soldier, combatant, enemy. Dispute, war, combat, battle, duel. Attack, defence, opposition, resistance, destruction, ruin, reversal. Enmity, hate, anger, resentment, courage, valour, bravery. Satellite. Employee.	**Intemperance**: Incompetence, ineptitude, silliness, stupidity. Imprudence, impertinence, extravagance, ridicule, inanity; swindle, fiddle, rascality, industry.
53	**Spy, forger**: Curiosity, observer, scrutineer, enthusiast, surveillant, listener. Examination, note, remark, observation, annotation. Speculation, tale, calculation, prognostication. Scavenger, artist.	**Unexpected**: Unforeseen, surprising, amazing, by chance, unhoped for, suddenly, to improvise.
54	**Tears** (10 swords): Sobs, moans, sighs, complaints, lamentation, affliction, chagrin, sadness, grief.	**Advantage**: Gain, profit, lucre, success; grace, favour, kind deed, ascendant, power, empire, authority, strength, usurpation.

No.	Upright	Reversed
55	**Clerical class** (9 swords): Apostle, bishop, abbot, priest, monk, hermit, religious, temple, church, monastery, convent, hermitage, sanctuary. Cult, religion, piety, devotion, rite, ceremony, ritual, celibacy, virginity, puberty. Recluse, anchorite. Vestal virgin.	**Justified distrust**: Well-founded suspicion, legitimate fear, mistrust, doubt, conjecture. Scruple, timid conscience, pure, timidity, decency, shame.
56	**Sharp judgement** (8 swords): Unfortunate position, critical moment, snap decision, miserable situation, delicate circumstance, crisis. Examination, discussion, research, blame, censure, gloss, epilogue, control; disapproval, condemnation, contempt.	**Indecision**: Difficulty, objection, contested, chicane, unforeseen, unexpected, chance case, venture, occurrence, destiny, fate, accident, mishap, disgrace, misfortune. Symptom.
57	**Hope** (7 swords): Waiting, desire, will, wish, vow, craving, taste, fantasy.	**Good advice**: Good counsel, salutary warning, novelty, announcement, notice, consultation, admonition.
58	**Road** (6 swords): Lane, path, way, progress, walk, consideration; middle, mannered, facet, expedient, course, career, promenade, dispatch, concierge.	**Explanation**: Publication, proclamation, obviousness, notice, publicity, authenticity, notoriety, denunciation, denotation, designation; knowledge, discovery, revelation, vision, apparition, appearance; admission, confession, protestation, approbation, authorisation.

No.	Upright	Reversed
59	**Loss** (5 swords): Shame, damages, prejudice, disadvantage, failure, route, reverse, ruin, debauchery, shame, defamation, dishonour, infamy, ignominy, affront, ugliness, deformity, humiliation. Flight, larceny, abduction, plagiarism, kidnapping, to steal. Hideous, horrible, dreadful, awful, appalling. Opprobrium, corruption, disturbance, seduction, libertinage.	**Mourning:** Regret, desolation, affliction, sadness, chagrin, calamity, mishap, grief, spiritual pain, burial, funeral, inhumation, sepulchre.
60	**Loneliness** (4 swords): Deserted, retired, hermitage; exile, banishment, proscription. Uninhabited, isolated, abandoned, neglected. Tomb, sepulchre, coffin.	**Housekeeping:** Good behaviour, wise administration, foresight, discretion, household, savings, avarice, to skimp, order, arrangement, rapport, conventions, concert, accord, concordance, harmony, music, disposition, testament. Reserve, restriction, exception; district, retention, wisdom. Symphony. Precaution.
61	**Distance** (3 swords): Departure, absence, distance, dispersion, background, delay, detain, repugnance, aversion, hate, disgust, horror, incompatibility, upset, opposition; unsociable, misanthropy, incivility, separation, division, rupture, antipathy. Section, break.	**Aberration:** Madness, straying, alienation of spirit, distraction, foolish behaviour; error, setback, loss, detour, distance, dispersion.
62	**Friendship** (2 swords): Attachment, affection, tenderness, benevolence, rapport, relation, identity, intimacy, convention, correspondence, interest, conformity, sympathy, affinity, attraction.	**False:** Duplicity, lies, imposture, bad faith, deception, dissimulation, deceit, misrepresentation, superficial, surface.

No.	Upright	Reversed
63	**Highest degree** (1 sword): Grand, excessive, outrageous, furious, quick-tempered; extremely, passionately. Vehemence, animosity, transport, fit of anger, wrath, fury, rage. Extremity, boundaries, confines, limits, end. Last, final breath, final extreme; tiff.	**Pregnancy**: Seed, semen, sperm, womb, swelling, procreation, conception, delivery, infancy. Fertilisation, impregnation, production, composition. Growth, enlargement, augmentation, multiplication.
64	**Brown man** (king of coins): Shopkeeper, merchant, banker, stockbroker, calculating person, speculator, physical, geometry, mathematics, science, master, professor.	**Vice**: Fault, foible, defectiveness, conformation, flawed, informed nature, disturbance, ugliness, deformity, corruption, stench.
65	**Brown woman** (queen of coins): Opulence, riches, auspicious, luxury, sumptuousness, assurance, surety, trust, certitude, affirmation, security, boldness, liberty, frankness.	**Uncertain, unsure**: Ambiguous, doubt, indecision, uncertainty; fear, fright, timidity, apprehension, vacillation, hesitation.
66	**Benefit** (knight of coins): Advantage, gain, profit, interest; utility, profitable, interesting, advantageous, important, necessary, obliging, unofficial.	**Inactivity**: Peace, tranquility, repose, sleep, apathy, inertia, stagnation, inactivity, idleness, leisure, pastime; recreation, insouciance, nonchalance, indolence, laziness, sloth; drowsiness, discouragement, annihilation.
67	**Brown boy** (knave of coins): Study, instruction, application, meditation, reflection, travail, occupation, apprenticeship, schoolboy, disciple, pupil, apprentice, enthusiast, student.	**Extravagance**: Profusion, superfluity, largess, luxury, sumptuousness, magnificence, abundance, multiplicity; liberality, good deed, generosity, charity; crowd, multitude; depredation, dilapidation, pillage, dissipation.

No.	Upright	Reversed
68	**The house** (10 coins): Household, economy, savings. Residence, domicile, habitation, manor, lodging, accommodation, hotel, palace, boutique, stall, lodge, shack, building, vessel, vase. Archive. Chateau, cottage, cabin, tent, pavilion, hostel, inn, cabaret, cork, tavern. Religious house, monastery, convent, hermitage, burial, tomb, sepulchre, cowshed. Family, extraction, race, line, posterity. Den, cavern, repairs, retirement. House of the zodiac.	**Lottery**: Lot, fortune, gambling, fortuitous event,chance, ignorance, fate, destiny, inevitability, stopping, decree, decision; dowry, legitimate, part, sharing, donation, gratification, pension, occasion.
69	**Effect** (9 coins): Result, consequence, evidence, conviction, conclusion; event. Execution, achievement, accomplishment, perfection. Possessions, furniture, real assets.	**Trickery**: Misrepresentation, surprise, error, lure, deception, fraud, deceit, ruse, pilfering, swindle, fiddle, infidelity.
70	**Brown girl** (8 coins): Honest girl, pleasing welcome, consideration, politeness, honesty, civility, complaisance, condescension, hospitality. Mores, character, nature.	**More**: Advantage, augmentation, majority, longer, much, copiously, abundantly; usury, exorbitance, exaction, with interest, avarice, more than, importance, elevation, height, pride, vanity.
71	**Money** (7 coins): Riches, sums, silver; silverware, whiteness, purity, candour, innocence, ingenuousness. Moon; purging, purification.	**Unease**: Tormented spirit, affliction, chagrin, worry, solicitude, care, attention, diligence, application.
72	**In the present** (6 coins): At the moment, presently, at present, now, forthwith, suddenly, just now, right away, in the hour, from the outset. Contemporary.	**Ambition**: Desire, wish, pursuit, cupidity, more, jealousy; passion, illusion.

No.	Upright	Reversed
73	**Male and female lover** (5 coins): In love, lovers, beau, husband, woman, spouse, boyfriend, girlfriend, enthusiast, mistress; to like, to cherish, to adore. Match, accord, convention, rapport. Fitness, propriety.	**Disorder**: Muddled, counter order, misconduct, trouble, confusion, chaos; damage, ravage, ruin, dissipation, decline; disturbance, libertinage. Discord, disharmony.
74	**Gift** (4 coins): Present, generosity, good deed, donation, gratification, service. White colour, lunar medicine, white stone.	**Cloister**: Enclosure, circuit, circumvallation, district, circumference, circle, circulation, to intercept, obstruction, engorgement, monopolising, imprisonment, arrest, settled, determined, definitive. Inflexibility, inexorable. Extremity, boundary, limit, term, end, barrier, barricade, partition, wall, hedge, fence. Obstacle, bar, unforeseen difficulty, suspension, delay, opposition.
75	**Nobility** (3 coins): Noble, substantial, important, grand, major, extensive, vast, sublime, renowned, famous, powerful, lofty, illustrious, quality; reputation, consideration, generosity of spirit, nobility of process, liberality.	**Child**: Puerility, infancy, childishness, frivolity, weakening, abasement, diminution, pettiness, lowness, mediocrity, meticulous, bagatelle, baseness, cowardice, rejection, petite, puny, rampant, vile, abject, humble. Abjection, humility, humiliation.
76	**Embarrassment** (2 coins): Obstacle, congestion, obstruction, trouble, problems, emotion, agitation, anxiety, perplexity.	**Letter**: Ticket, written, script, sacred text, profane text, literature, doctrine, erudition, work, book, production, composition. Alphabet, elements, principles, bill of exchange.

No.	Upright	Reversed
77	**Complete satisfaction** (1 coin): Felicity, happiness, rapture, enchantment, ecstasy, marvels. Perfect contentment, utter joy, inexpressible pleasure, red colour, perfect medicine, solar medicine, polished stone.	**Bag full of money**: Sums, capital, principal; treasure, riches, opulence. Scarce, dear, precious, inestimable.

Translator's Notes

General Remarks

The German translation excludes all reference to Etteilla (including authorship) and thus omits parts where Etteilla talks explicitly about himself. This may have been because of the antipathy of the German people for France at the time or an attempt to get away with effectively plagiarising Etteilla. Note that the French edition was published during the time of the French Revolution, and the first German edition came out only a few years afterwards (and the German edition this translation came from was published within a decade of the German states own revolutionary period).

The First Placement

Etteilla does not give any detail on how the cards are to be dealt into the rows, i.e. whether the first row should be dealt out, then the second row, etc., or whether cards should be dealt one at a time to each row. In another work[1], he suggests a procedure equivalent to the latter.

With regards to interpretation, Etteilla's big hint is that the three parts relate to levels of experience:

26 = spiritual; 17 = intellectual; 11 = physical.

And the remainder of the cards represent life, which explains the provisional nature of the reading (i.e. the role of free will). Specific hints on different combinations of cards is given in the second lesson from page 28 on. Here Etteilla also

---

1 *Manière de se récréer avec le jeu de cartes nommées tarots: pour servir de troisième cahier a cet ouvrage* (1783, 28–29).

hints that he favours an intuitive approach to interpreting the cards from their artwork over the use of divinatory meanings.

A paragraph worth meditating on is:

> Only God has created the entire universe, and the law written down in it — *that we shall find everything when we react to it and strive after it.*

The Second Placement

The procedure of redrawing (page 31) seems to imply either a swapping of the order (and discarding of the middle card) or a pairing of cards for interpretation, or both? However, Etteilla emphasises more than once that the order of interpretation is right to left. The procedure used in the example given in the Fourth Lesson on dream interpretation suggests that a pairing of cards is the intended approach.

The Third Placement

A point to remember:

> "the third time of placing the cards cannot be as certain and dependable for the science of oracle giving as the second time"

For the third placement of cards you need a rather large table or open floor space.

The remarks on page 39 suggest that as well as representing the past, present and future, the order of placement within each 11 has a temporal aspect. That is, the cards placed earlier in each 11 are temporally earlier than the cards placed later. Note also that it would be simpler and less confusing to place cards 12 to 22 from the top down rather than the bottom up — that way the pairing with the cards from the circle 56 to 66 would be easier and less prone to error. Whether there was a reason why Etteilla chose to place cards 12 to 22 from the bottom up and thus force a cross-wise pairing with 56 to 66 is something to meditate on.

Etteilla jumps from talking about interpreting the cards from the third placement in pairs to interpreting cards in sets of three. How these sets of three relate to the various placements is not explained.

The other combinations for the example are presumably:

1, 31 Gold, (44 Future) Λ, 34 Displeasure, 1.
1, 31 Gold, Λ, 34 Displeasure, (44 Future) 1.
1, (44 Future) 31 Gold, Λ, 34 Displeasure, 1.
1, (44 Future) 34 Displeasure, Λ, 31 Gold, 1.

The examples for the combination of the first three cards of the deck (page 42 ff.) are worth meditating on. Etteilla seems to be suggesting that this 'approach' can be extended to reading an entire row:

> For the way of reading three cards shows us how we must read four cards and up to the greatest number 26 which can lie in a row.

In the French edition, Etteilla comments that to say more he would only be repeating what he wrote in the work *Le Tharoth* (2 vol.). I have been unable to locate a copy of a two volume work of this name – though it may refer to 'the cahiers', of which he elsewhere (as noted) cites the third: *Manière de se récréer avec le jeu de cartes nommées tarots: pour servir de troisième cahier a cet ouvrage* (1783).

The Fourth Placement

This is the "strongest", perhaps as much because it is focused on a particular question. But note that the question may not be answered by the cards, and multiple attempts may be not enough – which points back to Etteilla's warning that God may withhold answers.

For the record, when I asked "Should I publish this book under the K A Nitz imprint?", the answer given was:

45, 7, 65, (49), 74, 23, (61)

The Fourth Lesson (Dream Interpretation)

Of note is the suggestion of using the cards to describe the dream in order of events, and then interpreting them by taking the first and last, second and penultimate, etc. The example seems somewhat contrived in that the reversed cards coincided in the reading.

Note that in the second placement of cards is was stated that with this way of reading any remaining unpaired card is discarded. This explains why the *gift* is not received – because that card is discarded as the odd one left over.

Key Words and Synonyms

The role that the astrological signs, elements and days of creations fulfill is not explained in this work.

Cards 13 to 17 each have a corresponding card that is the 'death' of them. So:

- 13 Marriage is the death of 14 Major Force
- 14 Major Force is the death of 15 Sickness
- 15 Sickness is the death of 16 Judgement
- 16 Judgement is the death of 17 Mortality
- 17 Mortality is the death of 13 Marriage

This sort of makes sense to me — marriage conquers all, strength holds sickness at bay, sickness impairs judgement, the Last Judgement (the picture on 16 of an angel with trumpets suggests this) or the judgement of posterity ends mortality, and death ends marriage. I suspect that these were meant as hints of the ways in which the cards condition each other's meaning/temporality when drawn next to each other.

In translating the synonyms, a number of concordances stood out:

- Anger: (2), 21, (40), (52), (63)
- Swindle/Fraud: 4, (38), (52), (69)
- Hermit/Hermitage: 8, (18), 55, 60, 68
- Sleep: (0/78), (17), (18), (66)
- Deceit: 18, 26, (34), (38), (51), (62), (69)
- Mishap: 15, 19, (27), (33)
- Happiness: 20, (32), (42), 77
- Honest: 22, 23, 36, (36), 37, (37), 42, 70
- Hate: (24), 46, 52, 61
- Grief: 19, 34, 46, 54, (59)